Colección Támesis

SERIE A: MONOGRAFIAS, 154

U.S.A. – SPANISH AMERICA

CHALLENGE AND RESPONSE

SOLOMON LIPP

U.S.A. – SPANISH AMERICA

CHALLENGE AND RESPONSE

TAMESIS
LONDON   MADRID

DISTRIBUTORS

Spain: Grupo Distribuidor Editorial, S.L., Ferrer del Río 35, 28028 Madrid

United States and Canada: Boydell & Brewer Inc., PO Box 41026,
Rochester, NY 14604, USA

Great Britain and rest of the world: Boydell & Brewer Ltd, PO Box 9,
Woodbridge, Suffolk, IP12 3DF, UK

First published 1994 by Tamesis Books Limited, London

Tamesis Books Ltd.:   ISBN 1 85566 033 4
Editorial Támesis, S.L.:   ISBN 84 88546 06 8

British Library Cataloguing in Publication Data
Lipp, Solomon
    U.S.A.–Spanish America:Challenge and
    Response. – (Coleccion Tamesis. Serie A,
Monografias;Vol.154)
I. Title   II. Series
970
ISBN 1–85566–033–4

This publication is printed on acid-free paper

Printed in Great Britain by
St Edmundsbury Press Ltd, Bury St Edmunds, Suffolk
for
TAMESIS BOOKS LIMITED
LONDON

CONTENTS

To sunshine
To music
To life
To Sylvia

PREFACE

This study has been occasioned by the observance of the 500th anniversary of the arrival of Columbus in the New World. The fifth centenary has stimulated a desire to examine the complex phenomenon known as America. What follows is a series of essays, independent of one another, yet connected by a dominant theme, namely, the "identity" of America, both North and South. "North and South" in this essay, are restricted to the United States and Spanish America, respectively. Brazil has been excluded from the discussion. "Identity" is an elusive quality which defies satisfactory definition, yet it is ever present, overtly or otherwise, like a continuous thread, as the reader progresses from one chapter to another.

One of the central themes involves the problem of perception. How do Americans, both North and South, perceive themselves and each other? How do Europeans view the Americas? The opening chapters deal with definitions and attempt to establish the limits of identity. With this end in view they utilize historical data to clear up the concept of "discovery" and enlarge upon the nature of colonization which accounts for the contrast between the two Americas.

Additional questions follow: What is "new" about the New World? Was it really "discovered"? What can be said about the attitudes and value systems which characterize the relations between North and South? Has there been a change in attitudes? The answer to these questions will vary not only from country to country, but also within the same country, and from one time interval to another.

The various perspectives concerning the "idea" of America, as well as the cross-cultural attitudes manifested, are illustrated by materials taken from *belles-lettres* and data located in the areas of philosophy, sociology and political science. Representative authors from both sides of the Atlantic, as well from the north and south of the Rio Grande, offer their observations and critical commentaries with varying degrees of objectivity.

The main thrust of the essay is the hope that the Americas will achieve a greater measure of understanding and cooperation, despite the differences in points of view and cultural perspectives.

All translations from Spanish to English are mine, except where otherwise indicated. For these I assume full responsibility.

S. L.

1

AMERICA: NOMENCLATURE AND "DISCOVERY"

Geographical terms applied to the various portions of the western hemisphere present difficulties of a linguistic nature which have their origin in historical and ethnic sources. To begin with, should the United States of America, properly speaking, be known as the United States of North America, since there are also other countries which bear the designation "United States" (e.g. Brazil and Colombia)? The citizen of the U.S.A. who has had some cultural contact with Latin America will often refer to himself as a "North American" instead of "American" in order not to offend sensibilities. Many Spanish Americans, with some justification, resent the fact that the Yankees have appropriated for themselves the name of the entire continent. They too, are Americans! Yet their protest, although valid from a logical point of view, seems unimpressive at times, since they hardly ever refer to themselves in ordinary conversation as "American", but rather as Argentines, Mexicans, Cubans, Nicaraguans, etc.

As a matter of fact, the term "North America" is also inaccurate, if applied exclusively to the inhabitants of the United States. A Canadian is also a North American, and so, incidentally, is a Mexican – all of which adds up to another frustrating instance of linguistic inadequacy. A U.S. citizen, travelling in Europe, will not refer to himself as a Texan, a Californian or a New Yorker to designate his nationality. If he is speaking English, should he say that he is a "United Statesian" (an awkward term at best)? But this would be inaccurate, since as already indicated, there is more than one country in America that calls itself the United States.

The terms used to designate the southern half of the American continent offer further complications. Those who opt for "Latin America" will find it difficult to exclude Quebec from this classification, since the language spoken in that part of Canada is derived from Latin. A further examination of the term "Latin America" will reveal that this designation was coined by the Second French Empire in the mid-nineteenth century to justify its expansionist policies in the New World. There are thus political and economic implications involved in the nomenclature which have left their mark in present day usage.

1

History is reflected in the term "Spanish America"[1] and may conceivably be linked with the colonialism of the past. In some quarters this designation at one time assumed ideological connotations. Many Spanish intellectuals, especially during the Franco dictatorship in Spain, emphasized the spirit of "Hispanidad" when speaking of the former Spanish possessions in the New World. "Hispanidad" stressed the religious values that go back to the Catholic Monarchs. The definition of Spanish America, according to this point of view, was intertwined with a sense of mission – that of Catholic proselytizing, coupled with the diffusion of the Spanish language and culture; in short, a point of view which speaks in the name of Spanish tradition.

Advocates of "Hispanidad" tend to look to the past for their inspiration. In this sense they are "traditionalists"; they utilize static elements of the past in order to justify their demands upon the present. If tradition is static instead of dynamic, it becomes traditionalism. Perhaps the Spanish traditionalists who harken back to the times of Ferdinand and Isabella do not realize that the Catholic Monarchs, ironically enough, represented in their day, progressive forces that brought about radical changes in the life of Spain.[2]

The term "Indoamerica" introduces a new concept. Coined by the Peruvian, Victor Raúl Haya de la Torre, it is symbolic of the expulsion of the Spaniard by the Indian. It can be said to represent a psychological necessity; it is anti-Hispanist because of resentment, and is identified with the struggle of the exploited masses against their exploiters. However, those who prefer to speak of Indoamerica, thereby eliminating the Spanish component altogether, are guilty of a dual error. In the first place, the Indians of America are not related to India. Secondly it can be said that the term reflects a "mestizo" mentality, rather than that of the Indian. If one bears in mind that Indoamerica purports to concern itself with the interest of the entire continent, such purpose would hardly be served by an ideology which is based on resentment against the white element of the population, a point made by the Spanish historian, Salvador de Madariaga. Madariaga emphasizes the Iberian or Hispanic influence as being the preponderant factor in the personality configuration of the many republics that comprise the lower half of the continent.[3] Yet it should be pointed out that the presence and influence of other groups cannot be ignored. What is called for is a synthesis of all the elements involved, such as suggested by the Peruvian writer Luis Alberto Sánchez, who maintains that the culture of his continent is Indo-Iberian. It is

---

[1] Those who speak of colonization by Spain and Portugal employ the term "Iberoamerica." For a fuller discussion of "American" nomenclature, see Edmund Stephen Urbanski, *Hispanoamérica, sus razas y civilizaciones* (New York: Eliseo Torres & Sons, 1972), Chapter one.

[2] Salvador de Madariaga, "Presente y Porvenir de Hispanoamérica", *Obras escogidas* (Buenos Aires: Editorial Sudamericana, 1972), p. 482.

[3] Madariaga, p. 480.

just as erroneous, he insists, to speak of the civilization of "Latin America" as to refer to the United States as "Anglo-Saxon".[4]

* * *

The question of nomenclature with respect to the emergence of the New World on the stage of history presents some interesting semantic problems. One must pause and take a second look at the "discovery of the New World".

What does the term "New World" actually mean? The word "new" is ambiguous. "New" in relation to what? "New" because the New World was discovered later? Later than what? Did the Old World become "old" only when the "new" one was discovered and not because it had grown old? Did the "new" exist before the "old"? The New World was new only for Europeans, claims Luis Alberto Sánchez. It is really the oldest world and made its entry into history "thousands of years before the Spanish, French, English, and Dutch established their respective communities".[5] From the perspective of the aborigines the Spaniards were "new".

As for "discovery", the term is a misnomer. Strictly speaking, the New World had been "discovered" earlier by the Scandinavians and the indigenous peoples themselves, who are said to have migrated from Asia via the Bering Strait. It is most likely that the Vikings reached the North American continent about the end of the tenth century. Norse literature credits Leif Ericson with reaching some part of New England or Nova Scotia during the early Middle Ages. It should therefore be pointed out that the invasion of the continent by the English on the one hand and the Spaniards and Portuguese on the other, can be said to constitute the "second discovery", as well as the first "conquest" of the New World. In fact, in many contemporary Spanish American circles one prefers to speak in terms of the "conquest" of America, rather than its "discovery".

In the view of North America, i.e., more specifically the inhabitants of the United States, the long-accepted tradition concerning Columbus's "discovery" was that the venture produced a country which eventually became a symbol of freedom and democracy, and a haven for the persecuted.

In recent years this version has been attacked as existing in the world of mythology. Columbus's journey, it is argued, was the prelude to an invasion. Europe conquered the indigenous people of the New World and destroyed their culture. Europeans brought slavery and infectious diseases to the natives. In more contemporary terms, the dominance of European values has

---

4   Luis Alberto Sánchez, *Examen espectral de América Latina*, 2nd ed. (Buenos Aires: Editorial Losada, 1962), p. 22.
5   Luis Alberto Sánchez, "A New Interpretation of the History of America", *The Hispanic American Historical Review*, No. 23 (1943), p. 442.

also resulted in the dangerous deterioration of the environment. In short, Columbus, according to this revisionist view, is not a hero but a villain.[6]

It cannot be denied that penetration of the hemisphere by the English, Spanish and Portuguese was violent and destructive. Hundreds of thousands of natives perished; countless numbers of Africans were subsequently brought over in slave ships because their labor was needed to replace that of the aborigines.

This attempt to re-write history may be viewed with a considerable measure of sympathy and understanding. Yet it would be appropriate to explore the motivations behind this altered perspective. Such an examination would reveal that the controversy is more germane to problems pertaining to the contemporary era than to 1492.

The second half of the twentieth century has witnessed an intensification of efforts on the part of native American Indians and Blacks to reinforce their cultural identity and assert their ethnic heritage. This would explain, at least partially, the attempt to emphasize "conquest" rather than "discovery". Laudable as this effort may be, it must be conceded that civilizations, empires, warfare and cruelty existed on the continent before Columbus came along. One should not allow an extremist position to obscure any long term positive elements which have resulted from Columbus's voyage. Any possible revisionism carries with it the risk of replacing one mythology with another. Taking note of the year 1492 should be an occasion for Americans, both north and south, to renew their efforts to make their world a better place in which to develop as responsible human beings.

History teaches us that Columbus, in search of a sea route to Asia, stumbled upon a land mass which he identified as Asiatic. In contrast, Americo Vespucio identified these same territories not as Asian but as something new and unknown. The element of novelty eventually qualified him as their discoverer and, hence, bestowed upon them his name rather than that of Columbus. Of interest, too, in this regard, is the fact that Columbus's son, Fernando, attempted to conceal the fact that his father had mistaken this new land for certain regions in Asia. Recognition of this error would have made it impossible to consider Columbus as the discoverer of the New World.[7]

The origin of the name America still gives rise to contradictory opinions. The popularly accepted notion is based on the explanation offered by the German cartographer, Martin Waldseemuller, in 1507 to the effect that the continent was discovered by Americo Vespucio. It appears that Waldseemuller was completely ignorant of the fact that the Vikings had explored the area hundreds of years earlier; nor had he ever heard of Columbus. Interestingly enough, Waldseemuller, some years later, was disposed to reject his earlier

6   "The Trouble with Columbus", *Time*, Oct. 7, 1991.
7   José Gaos, *Filosofía mexicana de nuestros días* (México: Imprenta Universitaria, 1954), p. 227.

assertion.[8] In fact, some authorities even go so far as to doubt whether Vespucio's baptismal name was Americo. Others believe that "America" is derived from "Amerisques" or "Amerricas", names of indigenous tribes of Central America.[9]

* * *

The "discovery", aside from historical consequences, can also be said to have provoked a good deal of philosophical speculation, since the concept itself tells us what Columbus did, not what he planned to do. The dilemma can best be expressed by the following question: Is the "discovery" of a "fact" independent of intentionality, i.e., of the idea of looking for something, especially if the two are not necessarily connected? In other words, is "discovery" *a priori* or *a posteriori*? Additional questions follow: Can one make a distinction between the idea of a fact, i.e., its interpretation, and the fact itself? Are there any facts which are independent of the ideas which we may have about them? Is the idea a necessary ingredient of the fact? In concrete terms and referring to the specific matter which concerns us: Did the "discovery" of America take place *after* the discovery of the unknown land mass?

It would seem futile at this time to attempt a mechanical separation between fact and idea. This would lead us directly into the firing line between idealists and empiricists. Perhaps it would be feasible to say that facts are not independent of ideas, nor are they reduced to ideas.[10] One may even venture the suggestion, and thereby put an end to this speculation, to the effect that the ideas themselves may be conceived of as facts which enter into historical relations with other facts.[11]

The basic question remains: If America existed as a "thing-in-itself" (and of course it did) before it was "discovered", at what point did it enter into the realm of historical awareness as America, and not as Asia? Our reference to Vespucio seems to provide the key. Whereas Columbus harbored the *a priori* thesis that the land mass he came upon was Asian, Vespucio, on the other hand, proceeded in *a posteriori* fashion. For him there was no previous "Asiatic" conditioning. The new, unexplored lands belonged to an unknown continent. Empirical evidence replaced previously held suppositions.

In short, it turns out that the "discovery" of America was an "accident" in the sense that Columbus was merely looking for India. The problem seems to be one which bears repetition: Is intentionality an essential ingredient of discovery? The Mexican historian Edmundo O'Gorman would reply in the

8 Jesús Arango Cano, *Estados Unidos, Mito y Realidad* (Bogotá: n.p., 1959), p. 15.
9 Arango Cano, p. 16.
10 Gaos, p. 249.
11 Gaos, p. 254.

affirmative. If the discoverer feels that there is something to be found, the discovery "by accident" is not really discovery.[12]

The nature of America's "discovery" may be viewed from still another perspective. The "discovery" may be linked to the needs and interests of the "discoverers". If one is to accept the premise that nothing is permanent and that, on the contrary, everything is contingent and circumstantial, then it must be concluded that America (both North and South) is subject to constant change. The nature of the continent is based on a series of concepts which attempt to explain its origin, geographical formation and historical evolution. These concepts are characterized by their tentative nature, since they are subject to continual modification.

For this reason, the very idea of America, in the interests of exactitude, should be couched in terms of "invention" rather than "discovery". If we return to O'Gorman, we find that he considers America to be a concept which was "invented", an invention related initially to the geographic entity and, subsequently, to its historical essence.[13] The Mexican philosopher Leopoldo Zea suggests a slightly different perception. America was perceived as a European creation. It emerged as a concrete reality from the cultural crisis which Europe was experiencing. The discovery of the American continent, according to Zea, had its origins in the unavoidable need which confronted the European, namely, the need to discover it.[14]

In other words, it is impossible to define America without comparing it to the western world or placing it within an historical context. The western world, at the very outset, i.e. in the sixteenth century, wished to convert America into a family of colonies and an instrument in the service of its interests. It is precisely because of this that it can be said that America was "discovered" because Europe needed it.[15]

---

12 Edmundo O'Gorman, *La Idea del descubrimiento de América* (México: Centro de Estudios Filosóficos, 1951), p. 20.

13 Abelardo Villegas, *Autognosis: el pensamiento mexicano en el siglo xx* (México: Instituto Panamericano de geografiá, 1985), p. 124.

14 Antonio Gómez Robledo. *Idea y experiencia de América* (México: Fondo de Cultura Económica, 1958), p. 32.

15 Abelardo Villegas, *La filosofía de lo mexicano* (México: Fondo de Cultura Económica, 1960), p. 155.

2

EUROPEAN REACTIONS

The emergence of the American continent – its shape, substance and possibilities – impinged upon European sensibilities with varying degrees of impact. Europe was to react, depending upon the differing motivations, with healthy curiosity, vivid imagination, adventurous spirit, hopes for the future, missionary zeal and shrewd calculation.

In the decades which followed its discovery, the idea of America, the image of the New World, became the focal point of numerous commentaries, learned and otherwise, advanced for the purpose of either substantiating favourite theories, guarded jealously, strengthening prejudices, or proposing utopias which would assuage frustrations and offer consolation for unfulfilled dreams.

From an historical point of view – and this applies to both Americas – America was seen as having evolved in terms of a dominant idea, a set of ideals which had always emphasized positive human values, hopes and aspirations. The human intellect has continually manifested the tendency to place in some remote corner of the universe an imaginary realm in which to construct societies, free from imperfections of all sorts, social systems characterized by utopian harmony. The new continent was to be such a state.

European reactions to the discovery of America and its inhabitants varied greatly. They covered the entire spectrum from admiration and enthusiasm to doubt, antagonism, and in extreme cases, calumny. For Rousseau and the Romantics, the American landscape was idyllic and unspoiled, and its inhabitants wise and virtuous. Cultivation of the soil, for example, would lead to true happiness which was to be found only in America.

In a way it may be said that Columbus was a precursor of Rousseau. He endowed the newly discovered nations with the lyrical qualities of the noble savage. Subsequently, Montaigne developed this Arcadian vision which would eventually find its way into the literature of Chateaubriand and Saint-Pierre. Montaigne contrasted the virtues of a primitive America with the decadence of a civilized Europe. The Indians he stated, "are in a state of purity; they are little corrupted by our laws. Lying, treachery, avarice and envy are unheard of".[1]

---

[1] Quoted in Arthur J. Slavin, "The American Principle from More to Locke", in R. L.

Nevertheless negative comments seemed to outweigh positive observations to a considerable degree. For example, the Abbé Reynal, who wrote *Philosophical and Political History of the Settlements of the New World*, promoted essay contests, the subject of which was whether the discovery of the New World had been a mistake. Some of the contributions were vitriolic in their analysis. Everything in the New World was corrupt. The men were weak; they had no beards and no hair. Their blood was cold and watery. Europeans were bound to degenerate upon contact with the indigenous population. It would have been better if Columbus had never set foot on the American continent.[2]

The eighteenth-century naturalist George Louis Leclerc Buffon, a contemporary of the Abbé, maintained that both the animals and the indigenous peoples of the American continent were weak and inferior because of the nature of the environment. America had only recently emerged from beneath the ocean, and had not yet dried out properly. Its humidity and decayed matter made for unhealthy conditions for both superior animals and civilized peoples.

The strongest attack came from Cornelius de Pauw. America was unfit for human habitation, he stated. It was primitive and unwholesome. Its inhabitants were little better than animals. De Pauw seemed intent upon unleashing a malicious attack upon the admirers of the Noble Savage. Buffon had spoken only of the fauna of the continent. De Pauw's vehement anti-Americanism extended to the nature of its people and its destiny. The American native was less intelligent and possessed less humanity; in short, he was degenerate.[3]

Because of the vigorous reactions to the theories of feebleness and degeneracy, both Buffon and De Pauw eventually were obliged to modify their initial positions. The latter admitted that the arts and sciences would flourish sooner or later, even in America – earlier in North America, because the English colonists "work with indescribable fervour to break up the terrain, purify the air, and drain away the marshy waters".[4] Buffon also altered his hypothesis concerning the degeneracy of nature in the New World, and spoke instead of America's youth and immaturity.[5]

* * *

Bruckberger, *Image of America*, translated from the French by C.G. Paulding and Virgilia Peterson (New York: The Viking Press, 1959), p. 148.

2 Henry Steele Commager and Elmo Giordanetti, *Was America a Mistake?* (Columbia, South Carolina: University of South Carolina Press, 1967), pp. 14–15.

3 Antonello Gerbi, *The Dispute of the New World: The History of a Polemic*, translated by Jeremy Moyle (Pittsburgh: University Press, 1979), p. 63.

4 Gerbi, p. 92.

5 Gerbi, p. 154.

Buffon and De Pauw had their Spanish counterparts. Early in the sixteenth century Juan Ginés de Sepúlveda had passed negative judgments as to the nature of the native population. In attempting to justify the Conquest, he resorted to Aristotelian arguments to prove that the natives were slaves by nature, and that the crudity of their minds made them subservient to the more elegant minds of the Spaniards. He sought to demonstrate that war was necessary in order to ensure the triumph of Catholicism, that the Spaniards were just in their dealings with the Indians, and that violence and slavery were justified. The natives were obliged to yield to the Spaniards and be governed by them, since the less intelligent are always ruled by the more intelligent. Had not Aristotle divided men into two classes: those who guide and direct because they have the intelligence to do so, and those destined to do the necessary manual labour? The latter were to serve the needs of the rulers. Appealing to the Greek philosopher to bolster his argument, Sepúlveda argued that the soul governs the body, just as man rules over the animal. Since free men rule slaves, their respective functions are reflected in their physical constitution. The bodies of free men are erect; the bodies of slaves are strong, robust and vigorous for the purpose of rough labour – a statement, incidentally, in obvious contradiction to that of De Pauw. In short, the more numerous class was condemned to slavery – a condition of servitude by nature (*a natura*). Only free men, the privileged citizens, could possess goods. To possess, then, meant to belong to the privileged class. Property was proof of social superiority.

But Sepúlveda encountered opposition. Bartolomé de las Casas argued that the Indians were indeed adept at social organization. Utilizing Sepúlveda's argument, he pointed to the fact that there were nobles, monarchs and men of property among the Indians. In fact, some of them owned slaves.

The argument began to become heated. Sepúlveda counterattacked: Indians were slaves by nature because they were barbarians, and they were barbarians because they were without reason. They were without reason because they were infidels. This argument was no longer Aristotelian; it was the Catholic faith or lack thereof which determined superiority or inferiority. However, argued Las Casas, Sepúlveda's position was contradictory. Religion was created for human beings, not for animals. Sepúlveda had implied that slaves were little better than animals. Condemning Indians for lack of faith implied that they were men and not beasts. If, on the other hand, they were condemned as being slaves by nature, then they could not be expected to have the faith.

At times the polemic assumed ludicrous proportions. The question of hairiness entered the picture once again. For example, ever since Biblical times hairiness had been associated with physical strength and vigour. The case of Samson comes to mind. A hairy man was a strong man. The Indians were therefore weak, since they were hairless.

This argument provoked considerable opposition in the person of the Mexican Jesuit, Father Francisco Saverio Clavijero. If De Pauw had seen the enormous weights which the Indians could carry, claimed Clavijero, he would not ascribe any form of weakness to them. Furthermore, according to the Jesuit, who had taught the Indians, they could equal the outstanding Europeans in the fields of theology, philosophy and mathematics, if taught properly.

However, old prejudices die hard. The original ideas of Buffon and De Pauw were repeated by William Robertson, the Scottish historian. In his *History of America* (1777), he referred to the cold climate of America; its inhabitants were lazy and their intelligence limited. The people of the Old World, he claimed, were far superior to the natives of the New World.

Another variation on this theme was echoed by Montesquieu. In his *Esprit des lois* he formulated a correlation between climate and character, claiming that in the warmer zones people were cowardly and enslaved, whereas in cold climates they were free. "The despotic empires of Mexico and Peru were located toward the equator, and almost all the free peoples were and still are to be found toward the poles."[6]

The polemic was also transferred to another plane. The Indian was no longer the subject for discussion. This time the argument involved the friction that existed between the "criollo" (the Spaniard born in the New World and his descendants) and the "peninsulares" (the Spaniards born in Spain). The Spanish Benedictine priest Father Feijoo jumped into the fray at this point. Taking issue with prevailing European opinion which considered the "criollo" inferior to the "peninsular", Feijoo rejected vigorously the charge that the creoles became senile before they grew old.[7] Many of them, he maintained, were actually of greater intellectual vitality than the Spaniards.

And so it went: charges and counter-charges. Manuel de Salas of Chile rejected angrily the accusation that the people of the New World were weak and effeminate. The Peruvian Hipólito Unanue criticized both De Pauw and Montesquieu, arguing that Peru's climate was temperate and that De Pauw's theories had no basis in fact.[8] Even the Abbé Reynal, who had considered the discovery of America a tragic mistake, was compelled to retract some of his accusations, especially those which concerned North America. Benjamin Franklin's scientific experiments compelled him to counteract his earlier charges of American degeneracy.[9]

One of the participants in the Abbé Reynal's contest was the Marquis de

---

6   Gerbi, p. 42 fn.
7   Benito Jerónimo Feijoo y Montenegro, *Dos discursos de Feijoo*, ed. Agustín Millares Carlo (México: Secretaría de Educación Pública, 1945), p. 30.
8   Gerbi, p. 316.
9   Commager and Giordanetti, p. 32.

Condorcet. Condorcet declared that the discovery of America was a blessing, rather than a curse. "America is a country," he went on to say, "of vast extent with millions of men preserved by their education from prejudice."[10] Condorcet speaks glowingly of the United States and of its influence upon the morality of Europe. Freedom to discuss is an antidote to prejudice. Tolerance brings about peace and prosperity. Europe can learn a good deal from America."[11]

The negative attitude evinced toward the inhabitants of the New World was not restricted to Europe. It was also manifested in America itself. For example, in the North unflattering references abounded. Protestants, such as Cotton Mather and Jonathan Edwards, doubted whether the Indians could attain salvation, or whether they were capable of understanding the gospel.

* * *

De Pauw's writings found an echo and probably reached their culminating point in Hegel. For the German philosopher, the New World was physically immature, the fauna impotent, and both its animals and inhabitants inferior. Hegel's opinion is probably the most quoted frequently. In his *Lectures on the Philosophy of World History* he states: "America has always shown itself physically and spiritually impotent, and it does so to this day..."[12] America has also become a place of refuge for the dregs of European society.[13] Elsewhere in the same text, as though peering into the future and wishing to counteract his initial negative criticism, he predicts: "America is the country of the future and its world historical importance has yet to be revealed in the ages which lie ahead, perhaps in a conflict between North and South."[14] The following statement is particularly irritating: "The people of Spanish and Portuguese America have still to emancipate themselves from slavery. They do not yet possess the spirit of rationality."[15]

As is well known, Hegel places the New World outside History. History, for him, is the Idea of Spirit, and America is still Nature, since Spirit has not yet been revealed or discovered there. History can only begin when the inhabitants of America have occupied the vast expanse of the continent; only then will spirit manifest itself. History is thus subordinate to geography. Hegel is kinder to the northern part of the continent when he concedes that it is less primitive than the southern half. America, speaking historically, is as yet only a promise, the land of the future.

10 Commager and Giordanetti, p. 39.
11 Commager and Giordanetti, p. 40.
12 Georg Wilhelm Friedrich Hegel, *Lectures on the Philosophy of History*, translated by H. B. Nisbet (Cambridge: Cambridge University Press, 1975), p. 163.
13 Hegel, p. 167.
14 Hegel, pp. 170–71.
15 Hegel, p. 215.

Nature, then, is the condition which precedes the appearance of Hegel's Spirit; the latter, in turn, evolves into the State. When Hegel was describing all the stages through which the World Spirit had to evolve – from the Absolute Idea to its embodiment in the Prussian State – he was chiefly preoccupied with the development of the Western World from its primitive beginnings. However, he had apparently overlooked the role to be played by the American continent. He was therefore obliged to correct this oversight and, consequently, sought to incorporate this huge land mass into his system of Universal History.

In short, America, according to Hegel, had no history; it had neither past nor present, which is to say that it existed only in nature, a forerunner to the realm of the Spirit. Man's spiritual potential could not function in mere geography; it needed history in order to develop. The New World existed in a time zone which could only be called pre-history. This pre-historic stage was the habitat of savages. Savages, like bees, termites and animals in general, did not have any history; they had only geography.

The Spanish philosopher Ortega y Gasset seems to reflect Hegel's ideas in his judgment of America as the land of the future and, therefore, promise. After his first visit to Argentina, Ortega refers to the promise of the Pampa, a geographic influence in the life of the Argentine. In this respect, he resembles Sarmiento, when he states that the barbaric Pampa has determined the character of its inhabitants.

However, this initial impression is soon modified. Following his second visit to Argentina, Ortega no longer stresses geography. Spanish America now seems to have entered history. It possesses a past, namely, that of Spain. The mother country has influenced the continent throughout the entire colonial period and, following that, for more than a century and a half after Independence.

Spanish America, argues Ortega, ignoring all other cultural and ethnic groups, is nothing more or less than Spain in some form or other, in its language, religion, tradition and culture. He thereby seems to contradict the initial myth of Spanish America as a "Promise", emphasizing instead, Spanish "historicity", its "nascent spirituality" and "healthy barbarism".[16] The Spanish American was, from the very beginning, a new type of Spaniard. Or to put it conversely: the Conquistadores were the first Americans. Following the same line of thought, it can be said that Independence was merely another example of Spanish separatism. The continent had not formally been admitted to European history, although geographic elements obviously marked its inhabitants as Americans. Even though Ortega seems to admit,

---

[16] Luis Barahona Jiménez, "Hispanoamérica en el pensamiento de José Ortega y Gasset", *Revista de Filosofía de la Universidad de Costa Rica*, 7, No. 25 (1969), p. 158.

after his second visit, that Spanish America is something more than mere possibility of being, he maintains that much remains to be done. This in itself justifies the claim that the continent is still the land of promise.[17]

Hegel had also affirmed that the Catholic Church had not kept pace with the World Spirit and that, as a result, Latin America had fallen behind vis-à-vis Europe's development. The Universal Spirit had by-passed it as Protestantism appeared on the scene.

Hence the Spanish American colonies, as the beneficiary of their Iberian heritage, were characterized by a dogmatic ideology in the religious area, and a quasi-feudal system of socio-economic organization. Spanish American society was not compatible with such concepts as bourgeois liberalism, private enterprise, individual initiative, etc. – all of these concepts which were associated with the rise of capitalism in the Protestant north of Europe.

Hegel's vision, almost clairvoyant in nature, recognized the potential friction between North and South America, precisely because of the contrast in social and political perspectives, shared in by each of the two Americas.

Worthy of note too, is Ortega's view of the State. The Spanish philosopher takes Hegel's definition of America as his point of departure. According to Hegel, states Ortega, it is necessary for people to live more closely together and to eliminate vast stretches of unoccupied territory in order to advance conditions that lead to the formation of the State.

Ortega pursues this theme even further. It is not so much the proximity involved in human contact, but the existence of a mass population that is important, since this would inevitably give rise to differences of social class and resultant discontent and conflicts. This represents the motive force which initiates the process of social history, a manifestation of the dialectics of Hegel's Spirit, which eventually gives form to the State as an expression of the dynamic of conflicting elements.[18]

The population factor brings to mind Sarmiento's attempt to populate and "civilize" the vast expanse of the Pampa. "To govern is to populate" was the slogan proclaimed by Sarmiento's compatriot, Alberdi. In this respect, the two Argentines seemed to be better informed than Hegel, at least as far as Ortega's interpretation is concerned. One may question whether population pressures by themselves necessarily lead to social clash and the consequent need for the State to come into existence.

One may prefer, instead, to adopt an optimistic view and maintain that the various sectors of the population tend to form social groups, which prefer to give their consent and support to the establishment of the State apparatus, if only to preserve the harmony and well-being of all concerned. It is in this

---

17 Barahona, p. 159.
18 José Ortega y Gasset, *Obras completas*, 2nd ed. (Madrid: Revista de Occidente, 1950), p. 575.

connection that such factors as "culture" and "civilization" come into play, and that the educative process considered by Sarmiento to be their most important instrument, determines the road to a progressive and democratic society, indeed to an America which would very much be part of history.

3

COLONIZATION: NORTH AND SOUTH

America's entrance into history coincides with the flowering of Europe's Renaissance. The idea of a better world, materially and spiritually, dominated the thinking of enterprising colonists from Plymouth to Río de la Plata. European thinkers of the period viewed America through Renaissance eyes. America, the land of promise, could perhaps, in the vision of these humanists, realize values which had hitherto not been attained in the Old World. The less idealistic motivation, especially for many Spaniards and Portuguese, was to enrich oneself.[1]

A new age had dawned. The medieval world was being replaced by Renaissance values. In fact, it has been said that the symptoms which signalled the dissolution of the medieval world were the elements which led to the discovery of America. The Middle Ages were not overly concerned with worldly matters; the medieval spirit was more closely identified with an aspiration toward heaven. This spirit was to give way to a period of conquest and colonization of foreign lands. In other words, the spiritually upward striving, the vertical perspective, was to be replaced by worldly horizontal expansion. The complete man, supposedly representative of the medieval synthesis which stressed all facets of human behaviour – physical, intellectual, emotional and spiritual – was to make way for the new type of individual, one that emphasized the here and now, and the desire for ego satisfaction which ushered in the Modern World. The Catholic totality was thus challenged by the thrust of individualism which found its religious expression in Protestantism and its economic manifestation in capitalism. In contrast to the Catholic component of the Old World which held that it was necessary to extend and enrich the medieval synthesis in the New World, those who rejected this perspective wished to create a new order in that world. Thus were the seeds planted in the two Americas about to be born.

And so the American ideal, at its inception, can be said to have assumed two forms: the Catholic group operated under the older medieval order and struck roots in Spanish America. It believed that all that remained to be done

[1] Waldo Frank, *Primer mensaje a la América Hispana* (Madrid: Revista de Occidente, 1929), p. 38.

15

was merely to fortify and further develop itself. On the other hand, the North American group rejected the medieval synthesis; it created its own system from the beginning. America was not going to be medieval but modern.

The men of the Renaissance yearned for a world free from impurities. They were dissatisfied with the socio-historical order which they had inherited, and aspired, instead, to one which was politically perfect and conceived in terms of rational formulas. One of several representatives of this school of thought, Sir Thomas More, who criticized European society of the sixteenth century, sought inspiration for his Utopian republic in the Platonic model of the primitive Christian community.[2]

The New World provided the opportunity for More's ideas to emerge from the realm of theory. Europe could not be salvaged because of old age. In fact, as one Spanish American essayist has put it: "God wished to recover in the New World that which He had lost in the Old."[3] The new man, naked and innocent, the recently discovered "noble savage", might be able to live in accordance with the dreamed of perfection, outlined in *Utopia*. In fact, More makes references to the natives of the New World and the voyages of Americo Vespucio. It remained for a Spaniard, Vasco de Quiroga, to attempt to put into practice what More had set down on paper. Quiroga, in his capacity as bishop and chief magistrate of New Spain, utilized the model he found in the *Utopia* to organize the Indian communities. For Quiroga, the natives of the New World were quite different from the Europeans. Their innocence, as contrasted with Old World malice, made them fit subjects for attaining a humanity superior to that of the European.

In this connection, the Mexican essayist Alfonso Reyes gives lyrical expression to the idea that the New World is a Utopian vision which has filtered down throughout the centuries. Reyes sees the American continent as an organism situated in time between a mythological past and a Utopian future. His vision views the discovery of the New World in terms of lyrical imagination, rather than scientific theory.[4]

Reyes's ideal America is that of a humanism which insists on perpetuating the cosmopolitan spirit as a means of fostering understanding among people. It is a missionary type of humanism which strives to incorporate America into Western culture and into the stream of universal history. In order to achieve this, it is necessary to establish links between the various levels of race, language and culture. This is the task of the intellectuals who must initiate and control the direction of the dialogue. Reminiscent of the Platonic ideal, Reyes considers the intellectual to be the principal actor on the Latin

2   Silvio Zavala, "La 'Utopía' de Tomás Moro en la Nueva España", in José Luis Martínez, *El ensayo mexicano moderno* (México, D. F.: Fondo de Cultura Económica, 2, 1958), p. 259.

3   Antonio Gómez Robledo, *Idea y experiencia de América* (México, D.F.: Fondo de Cultura Económica, 1958), p. 30.

4   Alfonso Reyes, "Ultima Tule", in Rafael Gutiérrez Girodet, *La imagen de América en Alfonso Reyes* (Madrid: Insula, 1955), p. 23.

American scene who will direct society's destiny.[5] Singing the praises of the New World, Reyes proclaims optimistically; "America is the stage on which all efforts to achieve human happiness will be played out. Today, in the face of the disasters of the Old World, America acquires the value of a hope... American culture is the only one that can ignore national and ethnic walls..."[6]

In short, human intelligence will rehumanize man. It will revitalize the source which made possible the socialism of the Jesuits in Paraguay; it will rekindle the utopianism of Vasco de Quiroga, and revive European dreams of America as the land of hope. For Reyes, the future America implies a better understanding of the concept of freedom, a more equitable system of justice, and a greater measure of happiness, in short a Utopia.[7]

The Protestant Reformation, having stressed the right to individual interpretation in religion, acted as a catalyst in spurring men on to struggle for political freedom as well. Linking this principle to the establishment of the new England colonies, it can easily be seen why the Puritans claimed to exercise freedom in both politics and religion. However, a word of caution is necessary at this point. One must distinguish between Pilgrims and Puritans. The Puritans were reformers who wished only to reform the Established Church in accordance with their beliefs. On the other hand, the Pilgrims, known originally as Separatists, were more radical. They wanted a church of their own. For them no amount of reform was satisfactory. The Separatists were subsequently forced to flee to Holland in order to escape persecution. However, this too, proved unsatisfactory. In Holland they faced the possible loss of their cultural identity, a circumstance which gave rise to their decision to migrate to the New World.[8]

The Separatists, or Pilgrim Fathers, arrived in Massachusetts on the "Mayflower" in 1620. This seemed to have been an accident since they had originally been bound for Virginia, but were forced to change course because of navigational difficulties. The Puritans, a much wealthier group, arrived a decade later.

The Massachusetts Bay Colony was founded because its inhabitants sought to escape from religious persecution and political oppression. For their inspiration and support, the Puritans looked to the Bible and the writings of John Locke. Locke had written his *Two Treatises of Government* in order to justify revolution which Parliament had initiated against the Crown in 1688. The Puritans, utilizing Locke's arguments, opposed both the King

---

5 Gutiérrez Girodet, pp. 50–51.
6 Alfonso Reyes, "Ultima Tule", in Carlos Ripoll, *Conciencia Intelectual de América* (New York: Las Américas, 1966), p. 424.
7 Gutiérrez Girodet, p. 52.
8 W. E. Woodward, *A New American History* (New York: The Literary Guild, 1937), Chapter III.

and Parliament. In their opinion, Parliament had refused to others the rights which it had claimed for itself.[9]

Yet this is precisely what happened in the new colonies. Despite the fact that the desire for religious freedom had been a motivating force in the Pilgrim and Puritan migration, dissent was not tolerated, once the colonies had been established. Roger Williams and Anne Hutchinson dared to deviate; they challenged the dominant religious principles of the power structure and, as a result, were forced to leave Massachusetts. Nevertheless, it should be pointed out that it was in New England that the main ideas which now constitute the basis of the social theory of the United States were first advanced. The immigrants brought with them elements of order and morality; they were accompanied by their wives and families. In contrast, other colonies had been founded by adventurers without families.

It should be noted in this connection that Virginia, the other early English colony, was founded by merchant adventurers who were chiefly interested in finding gold or precious stones. In contrast to the Massachusetts experience, English servant girls were eventually sent by the London Company (which subsequently became the Virginia Company) as wives for the colonists. In matters of religion, the Virginians were not so entangled as the Puritans. They were inclined to adhere to their established Church of England as a mere formality, and were content to let nature take its course. In a political sense they were the first to introduce a representative assembly in U.S. history – the House of Burgesses, in 1619.[10]

Comparing the colonization of the two Americas would reveal the fact that the Puritans had left their mother country, determined never to return; the Spanish conquistadores left only temporarily, intending to go back to Spain. The Pilgrims sought to build a new life for themselves in the New World. The Conquistadores remained loyal to the "madre patria"; they were more interested in transplanting the Old World – the social, political and religious structures – than in creating new ones. And yet they did create. Unlike the Pilgrims, they came without their wives. After having subdued the native population, the Spaniards created a new race, the "mestizos", which brought in its wake a host of socio-economic problems. By contrast, England did not admit racial mixture; racial "purity" was emphasized. Miscegenation was held to be a mortal sin. The presence of women in the English colonies helped reinforce the taboo against social and sexual intercourse with the indigenous population.

Octavio Paz utilizes the terms "inclusive" and "exclusive" to describe the difference between the two systems of colonization. Whereas the attitude of the Catholic Spaniards was "inclusive', that of the English Protestants was

---

[9]   R. L. Bruckberger, *Image of America*, translated from the French by C. G. Paulding and Virgilio Peterson (New York: The Viking Press, 1959), p. 24.

[10]   W. E. Woodward, *A New American History* (New York: The Literary Guild, 1937), p. 38.

"exclusive". In the first instance, the idea of conquest and domination was closely allied to conversion and racial hybridization, if not absorption. By contrast, the colonization in the North did not bring with it conversion of the natives, but rather their complete separation.[11]

The very nature of the native population contributed to the contrast. The English colonists encountered small, isolated groups of Indians. Unable to convert them into a labor force to be utilized, they preferred to drive them toward the west and south until they finally confined them to the reservations which have remained with us until the present day. In Spanish America, by contrast, the Indian population, generally speaking, was much more numerous and settled in substantial political units, characterized by a superior type of social organization (e.g., Mexico and Peru), which were subsequently taken over by the Spaniards. In this connection, too, it should be remembered that much more is known about the cultural attainments of the Incas, Mayas and Aztecs than about the indigenous people of North America. The Spanish colonizers undoubtedly produced a different personality type upon amalgamating with the indigenous population, not only racially, but also psychologically and culturally, as contrasted with the English and Dutch colonists who avoided contact with the natives. In this sense the present-day Spanish American can be said to possess more of an American past than the descendants of the North American colonist.[12]

If one were given to speculation, it could be said that Providence had put the law of compensation into effect at the beginning of the sixteenth century. Just as the feudal order was dying in Europe, it obtained a new lease on life, since its practices were transferred to the Spanish part of the New World in the form of large landholdings, cared for by what were virtually Indian serfs. Secondly, just as Catholicism found itself threatened by a rival sect, set in motion by Martin Luther, a New World was revealed, which contained untold numbers of souls to be saved by the Catholic Church, thus compensating for the losses sustained in Europe.

The contrast between the two worlds can be viewed from yet another perspective. It would not be amiss to suggest that in the medieval world everything and everyone occupied a definite niche in society, thus making for a harmonious and self-ordered whole, at least in theory. The modern world upset this well-established plan. The changing order tended to reward the spirit of individualism; every man could now effect his own, independent order. Protestantism and new developing commercial interests ushered in a policy of voluntarism and aggressiveness. No longer was man content to 'know his place' and be part of a harmonious structure. The social and

11 Octavio Paz, *Tiempo nublado* (Barcelona: Seix Barral, 1983), p. 147.
12 Américo Castro, *Iberoamérica*, 3rd rev. ed. (New York: Holt, Rinehart and Winston, 1954), pp. 5–6.

intellectual forebears of the English colonies can perhaps be said to best represent this individualistic spirit.

This is not to say that the Spanish Conquistadores and colonizers were entirely devoid of the desire for economic gain. However, it cannot be denied that the Spanish crown sought to bring to the New World its entire configuration of medieval religious values. Or, at least, as has been suggested, religious proselytizing was utilized as an instrumentality to cover up the desire for economic gain.

To offer a more balanced view, perhaps it would not be too farfetched to suggest that the Conquistadores stood on the threshold that separated two worlds. On the one hand, they were imbued with the religious values of the mother country, aided in their task by the countless number of missionaries who accompanied them. On the other hand, they were touched by the Renaissance spirit of adventure, audacious and enterprising – qualities which thrust them over the boundary line into the Modern Age. The Spanish Conquistador can be said to have possessed something of the adventurous knight-errant, although it would be more accurate to say that he was a mixture of the quixotic and the barbaric. Add to this the proselytizing element, as exemplified by "the cross and the sword", and it can be asserted that the conquest of the New World represented a combination of "the spirit of the Middle Ages and the vital humanism of the Renaissance".[13]

Symbolically, therefore, it can perhaps be suggested that a dying medieval world prepared the ground for the discovery of America, and newly-emerging, social elements made this discovery possible. America was thus the expression of a desire, the symbol of a need that demanded satisfaction.

The European Renaissance had led to the Reformation. Luther hatched the egg that Erasmus had laid, and Europe was split in two. Protestantism was identified with the "modern" nations; its spirit was adopted by North America, characterized by freedom of the individual, a greater measure of political democracy, and a desire for economic improvement. On the other hand, Catholic Spain and Portugal attempted to maintain the older status quo and, as a result, were left on the periphery of "modern" Europe. The Iberian legacy was to place Spanish America on a collision course with the northern part of the hemisphere.

European rivalries spilled over into the New World. Both Spain and England vied for control of the newly discovered continent. The conflict between them, which had its origins in economic motives, was cloaked and justified in religious terms. England condemned Catholicism as a mass of superstition. Spain did likewise vis-à-vis Protestantism. As in all wars, the issues were defined in terms of black and white.

The geographical factor should also be taken into account when one

---

[13] Jorge Mañach, "El Quijotismo y América", in *El Ensayo Actual Latinoaméricano*, ed. E. Mejía Sánchez and F. Guillén (México: Ediciones de Andrea, 1971), p. 94.

considers the problem of colonization. It has been asserted that Spanish America, extending from Mexico to Patagonia, largely desert-like in nature, offered a much less hospitable climate for colonists than did the North American seaboard. The Latin American continent, more tropical and mountainous than the United States, and with fewer fertile areas, is farther removed from Europe. In fact, the United States is more like Europe – whereas South America resembles Africa.[14]

* * *

A further contrast between the English and Spanish colonies is worthy of note. Rather than look upon the original thirteen colonies as a homogeneous unit, it would be more accurate to describe them as thirteen separate entities, each with its own characteristics. For example, the Dutch migrated to New Amsterdam which eventually became New York; the English settled in New England, the Irish in Boston, and the Germans in Pennsylvania. When these diverse colonies, dissimilar in origin and development, finally pooled their efforts, they gave birth to a national entity with a common purpose.

On the other hand, the Spanish colonies exemplified the process in reverse. Four vice-royalties were transformed into twenty republics after Independence. Local interests prevailed and fragmentation was the result. Larger racial units proliferated into sub-ethnic groups. A feeling of national awareness and continental unity was not allowed to develop. The colonies in the North established a federal republic and forged a national unity. Those in the South fragmented their cultural unity and established a score of separate political and geographical entities, victimized by one another's aggressive designs as well as warlike intentions by foreign powers.[15]

In this connection Salvador de Madariaga believes that if the national evolution of the Spanish kingdoms (Madariaga prefers the term "reinos" as opposed to "colonies"), characteristic of the North American territory, had been allowed to mature under the auspices of a civilized monarch, the rupture with the mother country would have been less traumatic. Unfortunately, the throne at the time of Independence was occupied by "the most dastardly king that Spain had ever had", Fernando VII.[16] This fact added more fuel to an already virulent anti-Spanish feeling, present at the time. Whereas the North American colonies adopted a system of regional and municipal governments in accordance with local sovereignty – more so than the pattern established in Europe – the Spanish colonies were subject to all

14 Mario Baptista Gumucio, *Latinoamericanos y Norteamericanos* (La Paz: Editorial Artística, 1986), pp. 10–11.

15 Eugenio María de Hostos, "El dia de América", in Carlos Ripoll, *Conciencia Intelectual de América*, pp. 151–52.

16 Salvador de Madariaga, "Presente y porvenir de Hispanoamérica", in *Obras escogidas: ensayos* (Buenos Aires: Editorial Sudamericana, 1972), p. 489.

the political and administrative errors imported from the Old World, and impelled to imitate the traditions of the mother country. The English colonies experienced no such compulsion. On the contrary, they felt free to create other forms of response to satisfy the exigencies of new, emerging circumstances.[17]

Whereas in North America there existed a general tendency to evolve toward the untrammelled examination of ideas and freedom of worship (although these were met initially by religious dogmatism and intolerance), the Spanish American colonies followed passively in the footsteps of orthodoxy to such an extent that the practices of the Inquisition were accepted uncritically until relatively late in the colonies' history.

Most of the English colonies were established, thanks to individual initiative, under the auspices of private mercantile companies. In fact, Georgia was the only colony founded by the Crown. On the contrary, in the case of Hispanic America, the mother country directed all the commercial and political activities. The colonists did not have to exercise their initiative. Everything was done for them.

The initiative exhibited by the early settlers of the North American colonies was to have a profound effect on their personality configuration as well as on succeeding generations. Their voluntaristic spirit was the stuff capitalism was made of, which would in the decades and centuries to follow, spill over beyond national boundaries and seek an outlet in Latin American markets. The expanding nature of the capitalist economy, characteristic of the North, eventually forced the America of the South to adopt a defensive posture. This was to be the case for the next two hundred years and was to perpetuate the conflict between the two until the present day.

Some scholars have taken exception to the oft-quoted distinction made between Anglo- and Spanish America, attributed to the fact that England went north and Spain gravitated toward the south; more specifically, that the two mother countries transplanted to the New World the struggle they had been waging in Europe. The Peruvian historian, Jorge Basadre, participating in a discussion more than half a century ago,[18] maintains that this geographical division, English Protestant North – Latin Catholic South, is not entirely accurate. For example, the Catholic Church in Quebec cannot be ignored although its influence has declined in recent years. French explorers reached important regions which are today part of the Middle West and South of the United States, and Spanish influence is visible in the Southwest and Florida. On the other hand, Germanic and Anglo-Saxon influences are strong in certain regions of Brazil, Chile, and Argentina. Despite their rivalry, England and Spain possessed some features in common. After all, the

17 Abelardo Villegas, *Autognosis: el pensamiento mexicano en el siglo XX* (México: Instituto Panamericano de Geografía e Historia, 1985), p. 126.
18 Jorge Basadre, *Excelsior*, Lima, June–July, 1942.

Roman Empire had extended its frontiers to the Iberian peninsula as well as to the British Isles. After the fall of Rome, many Germanic societies, influenced by Roman culture and Christianity, made their appearance. Europe as a whole represented a point of view quite different from that of an Oriental or an African. No matter how different Spanish is from English, they are both far more different from Japanese.

In evaluating the aims and outcomes of European colonization, it must be said that, regrettably, the dream harbored by the colonizers was not realized entirely. Human frailties derailed the best-laid and well-intentioned plans. In Spanish America government officials were corrupt and landowners were cruel and unscrupulous. In North America the Puritans established authoritarian theocracies. However, in each case the flame of conscience was not allowed to be completely extinguished. If North America had its Roger Williams and Anne Hutchinson, Spanish America could boast of Bartolomé de las Casas.

Nevertheless, America continued to be the land of hope and promise. For some it was an adventure and an opportunity for daring exploits. It beckoned to brave and restless souls to come in search of fame and fortune. For others it provided a scenario for proselytizing missionaries. Yet America also served to inspire those who sought escape from a continent rife with national and religious wars. These wars resulted in the rise of minorities which now had to make a choice: acceptance of the status quo or exile in order to be true to their faith and pursue their political aspirations.

To sum up: From a socio-economic point of view, the immigrants in the North represented a more advanced social structure, the result of a capitalist order in gestation. The Spaniards, by contrast, were the last representatives of a dying feudal system. The British colonists were prepared to found a new type of economy; the Conquistadores came to plunder and dominate.

The early colonizers thus diverged in their conception as to the direction in which they wished to see their homeland develop. Spanish America was the historical result of a traditional Europe, a Europe which looked upon itself as a complete historical reality, with no possibility of opening up to new horizons. On the other hand, North America (more specifically, Anglo-Saxon America) was not merely a copy of an old model. It was, instead, a European province which did not hesitate to try out new ideas and develop new avenues of development. Spanish America remained as a mere possibility. The United States did not apply European solutions to its problems; it created its own. It was therefore not to be wondered at that when the colonial period came to an end, the Spanish American was faced with a new giant that had emerged in the North.[19]

Yet despite the positive perspective presented above from which the

19 Abelardo Villegas, "El significado político del pensamiento de Edmundo O'Gorman", in *Cultura y política en América Latina* (México: Editorial Extemporáneos, 1978), pp. 49–50.

United States has been viewed, such an approach must be tempered with somewhat more realistic commentary. Even though the North American colonies had freed themselves of the illusion that all was well in the Old World – and had done so earlier than their Spanish American counterparts – they had not cast off entirely the European intellectual, theological, and political baggage, an impediment which prevented them from building their New Zions. They had rebelled against medievalism, but essentially their posture had not changed very much. As has been indicated, the Puritans were authoritarian and were bound to evoke a reaction in the form of the liberal tendencies that developed subsequently.

4

ESSENCE AND IDENTITY

As in the case of "discovery", one encounters difficulties in attempting to define the term "essence" or "identity". This is so because the process of describing the "essence" of America can be realized only in terms of studying and analyzing something or someone that is American. But in order to do this successfully, it is necessary to know that this object or individual is actually American, i.e., in contrast to someone or something that is not. To know this with certainty is to be aware of what is "American". The process then, results in a frustrating circle.

It seems, then, that we find ourselves trapped in a philosophical dilemma. Some of those who speak in terms of identity, think they will arrive at a satisfactory formulation if they analyze "essence". But what is essence? Spanish American essence, for example, as an *a priori* concept, does not stand up because it depends on Spanish American human beings whose characteristics have to be described and analyzed. And human beings are not objective, disembodied substances. They are moulded by experience, circumstances and history. Spanish American essence, then, cannot be objective. The hoped for *a priori* quality becomes subjective; it changes according to circumstance. We cannot transcend subjectivism. Spanish American identity, or any other kind for that matter, is not an abstract invention, nor is it merely the result of an act of self-contemplation. It is, rather, the result of dynamic action, a process of self-realization, a resolution of conflicts involving different problems.

From a metaphysical perspective, one runs the risk of speaking of American "essence" as though America were a "thing-in-itself", that is, as though it were possessed of a structure total and unchangeable. Yet the problem is historical rather than metaphysical. America is not a "Ding-an-sich", an unalterable fact or entity. History is not composed of facts, but deals instead with what we understand to be facts. History gives meaning to facts. The discovery of America is the *idea* which historians have developed, a suggestion already alluded to in connection with the viewpoint expressed by Edmundo O'Gorman. In the case of Columbus, for example, historians

25

may even have attributed to him situations which he himself never entertained.[1]

The essence of man's humanity is historical experience. Every man, at a
given moment, affirms his humanity through history. History itself is, thus,
the result of a series of affirmations and negations, of depersonalization and
humanization. To capture this historical sense is to be aware of the intercon-
nectedness of humanity. This human awareness is exemplified in the history
of America.

American essence changes and affects man in the process, and man,
likewise, undergoes change. This is the result of an historical process. Historical facts are thus necessary; without them, man has no history and does
not change.

Yet there is a risk involved. One must bear in mind that attributing
meaning to historical phenomena carries with it the danger of incurring a
considerable degree of subjectivism. Again we are faced with the dilemma:
historical data do not exist "in themselves", but only by virtue of their
significance bestowed upon them by human consciousness.

What does the idea of America represent in the course of its historical
trajectory? What America is has validity only in accordance with what
historical awareness judges it to be. In short, what it is, is equivalent to what
the idea of it is. It is difficult indeed to attempt to define American essence,
since the continent consists of an almost infinite diversity of peoples, cultures and histories.

If, in our attempt to define essence, we try to apply a system of axiological
categories (e.g., truth, beauty, goodness, justice), we are faced immediately
with a real difficulty: each of the above-mentioned categories contains a
multitude of different meanings. Which is to be selected as the only valid
one? In other words, the attempt to judge the historical process of Spanish
America, for example, by utilizing the norms of beauty and progress, etc., in
our endeavor to arrive at its value system, is a futile exercise if we do not
explain the content of these concepts.[2]

There is still another philosophical aspect involved when one discusses
the essence of the continent. If America was conceived originally as an
extension of Europe, or created in Europe's image, then we are confronted
by a curious paradox: the more America gets to be like Europe, the more it
ceases to be itself. In short, by becoming it stops being. Of course, this line
of thinking is based on the premise that America possesses a complete being
and structure. America is here conceived of as a "thing-in-itself". As has
been noted above, this viewpoint is anti-historical. It does not allow for
dynamic development caused by contact and interaction. The point must be

1   Abelardo Villegas, *La filosofía de lo mexicano* (México: Fondo de Cultura Económica,
1960), p. 198.
2   Villegas, *La filosofía de lo mexicano*, pp. 208–09.

made once again: it is not imitation of Europe that is the issue, but rather the principle of selection: selection of what is to be emulated for the good of America.

If one were to say that in the process of emulation America will stop being America, there is always the counter-argument: when a European culture trait crosses the Atlantic and reaches America, it eventually stops being European.

Within the philosophical framework, too, some Spanish American philosophers have questioned in recent decades the commonly held belief in the European Renaissance ideal of the New World as a Utopia. Leopoldo Zea, in particular, has challenged this view, maintaining that Europeans endowed the American continent with qualities, in accordance with their interests, ambitions and frustrations. In Zea's perspective, his America is a continent characterized by dependency and marginality. A European Utopia is still European and America cannot be a foreign Utopia. It has to create its own projects and implement programs which emerge from its own reality.[3]

* * *

The quest for and examination of one's culture or national identity has become a popular academic exercise in recent decades. Radio and television programs, publications and learned societies, have devoted what seem to be limitless amounts of time, space and energy to discussions dealing with the so-called essence, character or personality type of the average inhabitant of the various countries which comprise the American continent. For example, studies in characterology have appeared which attempt to analyze the nature of the Argentine, the Mexican and the Costa Rican.

Perhaps this apparent obsession with one's cultural origins can be related to epochs characterized by crises of values. A crisis may be caused by an over-emphasis on materialistic and technological values, and psychologically speaking, to the detriment of the human personality. In the economic sense it may be the result of imperialistic expansion which is inevitably associated with the exploitation of human beings. In such circumstances, not only individuals, but also specific groups and indeed, entire nations, may seek explanations for their predicament, or pause to analyze and evaluate what they conceive to be their cultural characteristics, their essence or identity.

José Ortega y Gasset has suggested a guide to behavior in this type of situation. In his book *En torno a Galileo*[4] he maintains that when crises occur, man becomes disoriented because his value system is questioned. In his anguish he begins to doubt his authenticity as a human being, which he

---

3 Leopoldo Zea, *Dependencia y liberación en la cultura latinoamericana* (México: Cuadernos de Joaquín Mortiz, 1974), pp. 48–56.

4 José Ortega y Gasset, *En torno a Galileo* (Madrid: Espasa Calpe, 1965), pp. 95–112.

feels is slipping away. In order to recover it, he finds it necessary to withdraw within himself, take stock of his resources, fortify himself spiritually, and face the world once more; in short, to renew himself, form projects and continue the struggle.

This condition and the proposal for its remedy may well be applied to an entire nation or group of nations, in search of solutions to their problems. Indeed, an entire continent which has had a history of critical experience may feel the need to define itself and take measures to realize its possibilities. Conversely, Ortega's suggestion may well be heeded by sensitive individuals or groups of individuals who live in a society which derives its comfort from activities that have a deleterious effect upon other peoples of the world.

The problem of cultural identity assumes a more complicated character in the case of ethnic minority groups who live in a dominant culture. This is well illustrated by the untold number of immigrants from Europe and Asia who have made their home in the Americas. Learning a new language and adapting to different cultural conditions may pose challenging socio-psychological problems, especially if the new arrivals wish to retain their native tongue and older culture patterns. The problem, in many cases, becomes more painful when the young generation, in its desire to acculturate, very often rejects the culture and language of the parents, considering these to be inferior and unworthy or unsuitable to the new environment.

At times the members of this younger generation may find themselves rejected by the dominant culture. They are now a marginal group, i.e., situated between two cultures, at home in neither, having rejected the culture of their forebears and not being accepted by the culture with which they wish to integrate. Of course, this classic example of an identity crisis is subject to a good deal of variation. It can be total or partial, i.e., contact with the dominant group can exist at the most superficial level, or not at all. Some people prefer to retain their centuries-old identity and withdraw into their own cultural circle of lifestyle and daily activity. The ghetto (Jewish, Italian, Chinese, etc.), enforced or voluntary, illustrates the point. Marginality can also be anti-social, as in the case of the Mexican "pachuco", living in California, so aptly described by Octavio Paz in his *El laberinto de la soledad*.[5]

The problem of identity is usually associated with such values as loyalty and allegiance to one's cultural group. Again, the problem of ambivalence comes up for consideration, as well as the emotional conflicts that result from such ambivalence. Sentimental attachment to cultural or ethnic origins often tend to interfere − although they don't have to − with the national identity associated with the country of one's residence.

5   Octavio Paz, *El laberinto de la soledad*, 3rd ed. (México: Fondo de Cultura Económica, 1963), pp. 9–23.

The sum and substance of it all is that we all possess several identities, in varying degrees. Realistically, we cannot speak in terms of only one identity, since our daily lives touch upon many aspects of human existence – ethnic, political and economic. There are regional, cultural and national identities. We are all members of various groups, primary and secondary; some contacts are stronger and more influential than others. The challenge that confronts us is to attempt a possible synthesis of all identities, effected in harmonious fashion, without doing serious damage to any of the component parts.

* * *

Cultural identity is often confused or equated with ethnic identity. This can prove to be an erroneous assumption, especially, for example, from the perspective of the native Indian. For decades cultural anthropologists have been speaking in terms of the desirability of integrating the indigenous population into the mainstream of Spanish American society and having it share in the "majority" culture. The question, of course, is whether the Indian chooses to "integrate". One cannot ignore the purely socio-economic component. Social class factors mingle and clash with ethnic elements, thus making cultural identity a far from lucid concept, especially in the Spanish American context. This is illustrated in the tensions between Indians and mestizos, and between mestizos and "criollos", as well as by the isolation of rural Indian communities. In fact, the very term "Indian" seems to be used in a cultural context, rather than biologically.[6]

Perhaps, in the case of the indigenous population, it would be more feasible to speak of ethnic, rather than cultural identity. Ethnic identity or ethnicity is based on an awareness of "otherness" and stresses "different-ness" with respect to other groups, whereas cultural identity is the result of a history and a language, common to the life of a given group, and emphasizes the preservation of its heritage. To illustrate this somewhat tenuous comparison: a homogeneous ethnic group may speak several different languages. On the other hand, there are different ethnic groups which share the same language.[7]

The various aborigines residing in Canada illustrate the point. They consider themselves the "first nations" of the continent, with their own identity, and do not regard themselves as Canadians in the accepted sense of the term.

At times cultural identity may be defined in terms of conflict, i.e., a negative attitude vis-à-vis another group. For example, the Third World may

6   See Solomon Lipp, "Racial and Ethnic Problems: Peru", *International Journal of Group Tensions*, 19, No. 4 (1989), pp. 339–48.

7   Jacques Lafaye, "Los abismos de la identidad cultural", *Past and Present in the Americas*, ed. John Lynch (Manchester: U.P. 1982), pp. 20–29.

share a common identity because of its antagonism toward another more powerful world. In the specific case of Latin America, definitions may not only be varied but contradictory as well. The Latin American continent is characterized by a variety of countries, social groups, institutions, cultures and sub-cultures. Consequently, the definition will be conditioned by the point of view of those who attempt to formulate it. Furthermore, the definition and image of Latin America acquire more solid substance when discussed from an historical and existential point of view, i.e., in relation to the Western World. It is only then that we can append such concepts as underdevelopment, dependency, Europeanization, universality, nativism, originality and authenticity.

Spanish America's on-going examination of itself seemed to produce erratic oscillations of the cultural pendulum. At times a well-nigh schizophrenic mentality looked to Europe for inspiration and sustenance; at others, it turned inward upon itself toward native culture and traditions in an attempt to define its essence and identity.

Servile imitation of European models has, in the past, produced negative nativist reactions. It is relatively easy to be anti-foreign or anti-western, if western influences are equated with foreign imperialism. It is a simple step to fall into the extremely nationalistic or chauvinist trap. It is all the easier if the Europeanized culture patterns have been adopted by a landed aristocracy or a powerful oligarchy. In that case, to be nativist is akin to being anti-imperialist. Xenophobia assumes a "revolutionary" stance. It should be remembered that identity can be utilized by various sectors of society to advance their respective class interests.

Any cultural, national or continental identity is, of necessity, a pluralistic concept. No one social, political or economic group exercises an exclusive monopoly over cultural values. The heterogeneous nature of the Latin American continent, indeed of any single country, as a result of its social, economic and ethnic components, obliges us to consider identity as a pluralistic concept and to speak of cultural identities in the plural.

Identity does not come ready made. It is in a continuous process of development. It has to be encouraged and nurtured, fought for, defended and secured. There are negative and positive motivations which serve to spur on a people to become aware of itself. In a dialectical relationship the negative will often act as a stimulus to inspire the positive. For example, in the process of achieving its identity, Latin America must resist certain pressures which stand in the way. Internal obstacles must be dealt with, as well as external or foreign elements which are all too eager to make use of these self same internal forces for their own benefit.

What has been said about the conflict between nativism and Europeanization (sometimes referred to erroneously as universalism), has its repercussions on the literary scene. Literature possesses both national and universal qualities. An exclusively nationalistic literature concerns itself solely with national or regional elements. A so-called universalist or cosmopolitan literature cannot exist *in vacuo*, divorced from historical or geographic circumstances. Both perspectives are erroneous because they are exclusivist. One arrives at the cosmopolitan via the national. *Don Quixote* is the most Spanish of books; it is also the most universal.

* * *

Generally speaking, the idea of national identity or authentic "essence" carries with it a multiplicity of variables, complications and ambiguities which require clarification. Above all, cultural and national (or continental) sentiment cannot be studied in isolation, divorced from other aspects of hemispheric reality. A number of other factors impinge upon the nature of identity, such as race, religion, language, history and psychology. Moreover, these may be reinforced by political and economic interests.

As has been noted, one's perspective also affects the definition as to who exactly is an "authentic" American. The answer will depend on the attitude, intentions and ideology of the individual being defined, or the person who does the defining. The temporal factor must also be taken into account. A sixteenth-century evaluation is probably not the same as a twentieth-century judgment. Furthermore, when we speak of America and American values, are we describing conditions and relationships which exist at present or are we projecting our hopes and aspirations for the future? Are we speaking of that which *is* or what can and *ought* to be? Is American identity a static or a dynamic concept? Are we emphasizing *being* or *becoming*?

The question of cultural identity, insofar as this relates to the essence which each of the two Americas claims to personify, or the idea which they have of themselves, is intimately linked to the national image or sets of values nurtured and cherished in the interests of survival.

Such terms as national character, nationality, nationalism and Americanism turn out to be concepts just as multifaceted and resistant to clear definition as the idea of cultural identity itself. Definitions of national character tend to merge with outworn stereotypes, whereas interpretations of nationalism vary in accordance with a particular social group whose uppermost objective at a given historical moment is the promotion of its political and economic interests. For example, nationalism may not refer only to the perception of differences between social groups, but also to the belief that one social group is superior to others.

Concern with national character generally arises with the appearance of what are considered to be crises of ideological dimensions. For example, preservation of one's national identity comes to the surface of Canadian consciousness in the face of "threatening" economic activity by the United States. Quebec nationalists, who strive to maintain their French identity, worry about elements that appear to jeopardize their security.

* * *

Numerous studies of American character, identity, personality or "essence" (both North and South) have enriched and, at times, distorted our knowledge of ourselves and our neighbors. Many volumes have dealt with the subject from a number of different perspectives. They have been merely descriptive, based on personal impressions, or they have utilized sources and methodology borrowed from psychology, philosophy, history and sociology. Yet despite the fact that these studies have added to the already overcrowded library shelves, there is still – as the Spanish has it – "a good deal of ink left in the inkwell", as far as the nature of America and the Americans is concerned.

There can be no more serious error than that of evaluating a nation, or a continent for that matter, from only one point of view, and endowing it with only one tradition. Within the same geographic area, considered as a national entity, there can exist as many traditions as correspond to different ethnic groups. For example, the United States plays host to the traditions of the English, Irish, Scots, Germans, Jews, Africans, Hispanics, Slavs, Italians, Greeks, etc.

The same can be said of Latin America. In order to evaluate the traditions of the continent, it is necessary to take into account the presence of the native Indians, the Spaniards, Portuguese and other Europeans, the Africans, Asians, Catholics, freethinkers, republicans, rural and urban inhabitants, nobles and plebeians, civil and military.

Usually, the concept of identity implies that one has to identity oneself with something or someone. We generally identify with a group or various groups, primary and secondary. Who, for example, can claim that he or she is an "authentic" American? What is "authentic"? Some additional questions follow: What is it that makes a Mexican? What differentiates a Mexican from an Argentine? What is *their* idea of a Spanish America? What does a Spanish American have in common with a Brazilian? What do Ibero-Americans have in common with North Americans? What is it that represents the idea of America in the first place? One should avoid the temptation to generalize about the characteristics of a people. This is especially obvious when one examines the historical trajectory of this people in the course of several centuries, and notes the changing circumstances and their effects upon the personality of the inhabitants. The North American, as well as the Spanish American, is today quite different from his forebears.

The vantage point occupied by a specific group will determine the image or identity of the nation or continent. Such perspective is conditioned by two coordinates: the vertical and the horizontal. These are associated with the socio-economic scale and the geographic factor, respectively. The position occupied by certain social and economic groups within the Spanish American structure will determine the choices and alternatives. Will the continent be satisfied to act as an *object*, receiving pressures from abroad, or will it reject this role and strive to become a *subject* which will exert a more dynamic influence? Specifically, one of the most vexatious problems at the present moment is political and economic in nature. Only by solving this problem can cultural identity be assured.

The fact is that in the contemporary period of rapid social change, objects are no longer content to remain that way. They want to act as subjects. The fact is also that some countries which have hitherto been subjects and have enjoyed the freedom to act in that capacity, are now reluctant to extend this freedom to others which are tired of being objects of exploitation.

In recent years studies in national identity or cultural characterology have progressed from intuitive impressionism to a more sophisticated perspective which makes use of an interdisciplinary approach, and attempts to utilize a more objective and scientific methodology. Nevertheless, this does not always offer or guarantee satisfactory results.

A basic problem which is not easily solved, still remains: Can cultural traits be isolated from national character? Or are the two intertwined? Is the cultural factor independent? If cultural traits are products of the socio-political structure of a given historical moment, can they be considered permanent? How can this be so if — as is to be expected — the structures are subject to changes, and the cultural factor is necessarily shaped by changing circumstances?

In the past, for example, the Western powers, especially the United States, have proclaimed the virtues of democracy, and have represented themselves as the bearers of humanistic ideals. In practice, however, according to Leopoldo Zea, they have appropriated these values for themselves.[8] Speaking as a philosopher, he maintains that his Spanish American colleagues should draw the necessary conclusions. Philosophy is not sufficient if it merely offers a conception of the universe. It must also serve as an instrument to discover the meaning and position of the Latin American world.

This does not mean denying the past or turning one's back on what Spanish America has learned from the European experience and circumstances. It does mean absorbing all that has been offered by the historical past, but in a selective manner. This is an especially urgent task at the present historical juncture when political and socio-economic struggles have intensified. The genuine humanistic values are to be found in the movement which has inspired the so-called philosophy of liberation. Philosophy, in this respect, cannot continue to be a mere explanation of the world, but rather a means to effect a transformation of that world, specifically, the Latin American world — a point of view reminiscent of Karl Marx's famous assertion of a century and a half ago, to the effect that the duty of philosophers is not

8   Leopold Zea, pp. 32–47.

merely to interpret the world, but to change it. Praiseworthy as this may be, it carries within itself the seeds of a dilemma of which we should all be aware. At the present moment, when axiological relativism seems to reign triumphantly, one should guard against converting a philosophical position into a matter of mere opinion. It must be recognized that there are certain universal values that transcend relativist frameworks, and which are worth fighting for, even in the philosophical realm, precisely because they are valid for *all* human beings.

Nevertheless, a concluding note is called for at this point. There is something to be said for the relativist posture. Philosophy cannot be considered as though it existed in a vacuum. It, too, like any system of thought which possesses a structure and a methodology, may be viewed as a reflection of ideas controlled by the distribution and functioning of social forces. It may also be an instrumentality to effect a transformation of such social arrangements. For example, a social class which occupies a dominant position in a given society and is interested in preserving that position, would tend to nurture and give support to a philosophic stance which stresses the value of the status quo. Such a philosophy, static in nature, would stress values of permanence and minimize elements of change. On the other hand, a social group or class which has been abused for decades, and occupies a lower rung on the ladder of social advancement, and which strives to change the status quo in order to improve its condition, would probably prefer a dynamic philosophy which emphasizes change.

It is in this sense that philosophic values become subjective and assume an instrumental character. Latin American philosophers can scarcely be faulted if they choose to embark upon a path which seeks to put an end to dependency and underdevelopment to which their continent has been subjected. The philosophy of the subjugated groups is bound to be different from that of the dominant elements. The differences will become obvious in the number and types of issues dealt with, the approach to these categories, the nature of the problems and circumstances confronted and the solutions offered, as well as the timing and methodology involved. It is conceivable that a philosopher who adheres to this kind of orientation may actually find himself in a dangerous situation – something that would not occur if he were a proponent of the philosophic school which stresses "static", "objective", and "permanent" values.

In comparing the philosophic currents of the two Americas, it would appear that the dominant tendencies in the North have been the influences exerted by the natural sciences and mathematics, whereas in Latin America the emphasis seems to veer toward the social studies. In this context it is not difficult to understand why the philosophy of liberation would take hold in Latin America and not in the United States.

Some basic questions remain: Is it possible to achieve "universal" values by way of a "relativist" approach? After all, it is possible to reach the mountain top from the valley below by means of more than one path. Some roads may be paved highways; others are winding dirt roads with an occasional detour. The former are smoother with fewer obstacles, but the latter may be more picturesque. Does a "relativist" value become "absolute" at a given moment in history, i.e., when it does not allow for the existence of other values, thereby ceasing to look upon itself as "relativist"? Can various points of view, each in its own way, strive to attain certain universal values, and thereby arrive at the grand synthesis? Thorny questions at best.

5

SPANISH AMERICA
IN SEARCH OF IDENTITY

The problem of cultural identity is related to national values and their observance. At times, these would seem to provoke more controversy than agreement. The relativism of the issues involved appears to hinder any semblance of consensus. For example, with reference to Spanish American identity: whose value system is more "national" and "authentic": that of Francisco Solano López of Paraguay, head of an authoritarian, theocratic regime and responsible for the most savage war in Latin American history, or that associated with Domingo Faustino Sarmiento, the "Educator-President" of Argentina, imbued with the doctrines of political and economic liberalism? Who is more "national": Diego Portales, spokesman for the conservative "pelucones" of Chile, or his countryman, Francisco Bilbao, anti-Catholic and fervent republican? Is José Enrique Rodó more "authentic" and "representative" of the so-called Spanish American personality or identity image than Victor Raúl Haya de la Torre, or for that matter, Fidel Castro?

Linking cultural identity with a feeling of nationhood can thus present a series of complex problems. To begin with, the idea of nationalism must be placed in its historical context and its variations explained before it can be applied to the theme under consideration. Clarity of definition is difficult to achieve because there have been different varieties of nationalism which have developed under changing circumstances. In the modern sense it usually involves a love of common territory, race, language and culture. It may also partake of a mystical quality, i.e., a vague and deeply emotional devotion to a social organism which is equal to more than merely the sum of its individual parts. The nation, in the modern sense, is identified with a sovereign government; it has a common history and believes in a future destiny; it fosters a state of mind (patriotism) in which the supreme loyalty of the individual is expected to be rendered to its political organization.

This political component, the nation-state, was born in eighteenth-century western Europe because it was essential to the economic organization of modern times. Its emotional component, nationalism, spread all over Europe in the nineteenth, and became a world-wide movement in the present century. Specifically, nationalism was a product of bourgeois society. The middle class saw in it the chief medium to realize its ideas. The interests of this class were identified with the interests of all of society, or the nation. The bourgeoisie believed that the ideal, liberal society could be established, inspired by the Enlightenment, with it emphasis on democracy. In this task the working class would be included as well. A popular nationalism was thus part of the general movement, republican, anti-monarchical and anti-clerical in nature, and representing John Locke's philosophy of the pursuit of happiness.

An additional factor must be mentioned in this connection in order to round out the picture. The growth of nation-states which was marked by the existence of national and/or cultural minorities within their geographic parameters presented further complications. Within these political structures, ways and means had to be developed which would insure the accommodation of the cultural aspirations of ethnic minorities to the culture patterns of the dominant national group.

* * *

The spirit of nationalism can also be utilized by different groups of society. It can be liberal or conservative, radical or reactionary. It can stress form at the expense of content. Symbols can become more important than essence. Nationalism can thus be progressive or retrogressive. This will depend on the stage of economic development experienced by the nation in question.

In the early stage, as has been pointed out, nationalism was an expression of struggle by the rising bourgeoisie against a social and economic system which had outlived its usefulness. Within a Third World context at the present time it has taken on the coloration of a progressive movement in the sense that it has symbolized the struggle of a national bourgeoisie against imperialistic powers. Middle-class nationalists aim at national self-determination. In this situation they very often receive the support of the laboring masses, both rural and urban, and of the political parties which claim to represent them. In the contemporary era, liberals and socialists tend to support Asian and African nationalists.

It should not be forgotten that nationalists and socialists (or Communists) have often parted company (e.g., in China) after having attained their common goal, because of a divergence of interests and purposes. It should also be pointed out that many leftists become rightists, thus causing the nationalist picture to become even murkier. A given political party often determines the political coloration of the movement. For example, the same nationalist tendencies in the contemporary world scenario may be considered right-wing by socialists if these are manifested in Europe, and a left-wing movement if they appear in Asia or Africa.

The latest manifestation of the dizzying course played out by the Communist-nationalist conflict is, of course, represented by the violent political changes that have occurred in the former Soviet Union and Eastern Europe. Nationalist elements have rebelled against communist regimes; communist governments, in order to preserve their power, have in some cases adopted nationalist verbiage. The upsurge of this nationalist sentiment is a reaction to a regime which had suppressed nationalist tendencies, considered a "bourgeois" threat to the Soviet state. Whether this nationalist manifestation is of a progressive nature remains unclear as of this writing.

In short, one must bear in mind that nationalism can be reactionary as well as progressive. When imperialist powers, for example, seek to extend their influence in various parts of the world, they will often utilize nationalist slogans to advance their interests. On the other hand, for those nations which find themselves in a subordinate position – former colonial countries which seek to emerge from their dependency status – nationalist urges and policies assume a progressive character and liberating function.

In Spanish America nationalist verbiage has served as a political and economic instrument in the hands of those sectors of the population which have striven to promote the nationalization of the industrialization and modernization of the economy, as opposed to those social forces (both internal and external) that are more interested in preserving the status quo, which implies a continued subservience to foreign economic interests.

Nationalism thus wears different guises: political, economic and cultural. These do not exist in isolation, but invariably interact and reinforce one another. Economic nationalism, for example, is a phenomenon associated with "underdeveloped" or "peripheral" nations (for want of a more suitable term); in other words, with those which have been subjected to the influence of more powerful, industrially developed nations.

Nations which are at the mercy of foreign investments and monopolies, and are therefore forced into a position of dependency and unable to develop their own industries, are fertile ground for the seeding and sprouting of nationalist movements. Such nations are also compelled to play the role of suppliers of raw materials in exchange for imports of manufactured goods. Foreign governments are reluctant to allow predominantly agricultural countries to develop industries which would make it possible for these poorer nations to enter the competitive world markets. They will therefore exert their influence to maintain the status quo and not "rock the boat". If necessary, they will exert pressure upon governments to eliminate or diminish potential threats in order to protect their own financial interests, and make efforts to effect favorable political alignments.

It is at this point that politics become a clear manifestation of economics. The reaction within the less favored nations on the part of significant sectors of the population assumes expressions of opposition to foreign expansionism, imperialism, transnational trusts and monopolies. Political activities thus become a reflection of diverse economic interests. Some political parties will attack the invasion by foreign capital. Others will favor the "invasion" in the name of the national welfare. Economic nationalism is thus metamorphosed and merged with political nationalism. All groups will claim to be authentic patriots and proclaim that their point of view is beneficial for the nation's well-being.

The situation is even more acute if an underdeveloped country is wholly dependent upon one or two of its chief products, for example, sugar or coffee, for its economic existence. In that case, prices on the world market may well bring a country to its knees. Nationalism, in these circumstances, especially in the form of jingoism or chauvinism, is a powerful weapon, utilized to rally the people in the campaign against foreign penetration.

It is relatively easy in Latin America to have nationalism develop as an outgrowth of anti-foreignism, especially if xenophobia is identified with anti-capitalism and anti-imperialism. Capitalism and imperialism are natural targets for the progressive elements of society and, as already stated, usually associated with the political left. However, right-wing military dictatorships, often supported, regrettably enough, by trade unions and mass organizations, have also been known to adopt nationalist policies and mouth anti-imperialist slogans. Populist movements in Argentina and Brazil, for example, identified with fascist ideology, have found themselves in bed with socialists and communists. The lines of ideological differentiation have often been far from clearly discernable and not easily disentangled.

A healthy nationalism that speaks in terms of love of country does not refer only to a geographical area occupied by a group of people. The geography is important because it represents peace, hope and security for these people and their descendants. The piece of land mirrors historical experience of which the inhabitants may well be proud. Above all, it does not represent, as so often happens, the sacrifice of the many for the benefits of the few.[1]

* * *

The problem of nationhood is a significant variable which distinguishes the two Americas. In the United States, as in Europe, the Nation makes its appearance before the State comes into being, or rather, the latter accommodates itself to the former. Experience and circumstance determine the nature of law; function and operation produce the organ. In Hispanic America the process is reversed. The State is born on the continent before the Nation takes shape. In order for a Nation to exist, it is necessary, so it is thought, to create the State.

In the pre-Conquest period there were Nations: Inca, Aztec and Maya. However, after these were destroyed by the Spaniards, the creoles, vaguely sensing the awakening national awareness, made use of the State in order to

[1]   Luis Alberto Sánchez, *Examen espectral de América Latina*, 2nd ed. (Buenos Aires: Editorial Losada, 1962), p. 250.

give it shape and encourage its development. They realized that the establishment of a new State would contribute to the creation of a national
consciousness. In short, in this case, the organ or the agent preceded the
activity. As Caballero Calderón puts it: "The army before the war, the law
before the crime, the written Constitution before the national awareness."[2]

Still one more factor needs to be stressed. In order that a country may lay
claim to nationhood, it is necessary for all who reside therein to share in its
government, its hopes for the future, and accomplishments of both past and
present. From this vantage point it is quite understandable for some critics to
maintain that not all countries in Hispanic America are nations. For example,
Victor Alba maintains that all elements of a country must desire freedom and
democracy, thus making these two goals necessary ingredients of nationhood. This is not the case in a number of countries of Spanish America.[3]

The point to remember is that since democracy implies power-sharing and
a more equitable distribution of wealth, the task of true nation-builders, not
demagogues, is to involve all segments of the population in the process, and
reduce to a minimum convenient alibis for not doing, or postponing what has
to be done. Looking for scapegoats, such as Yankee imperialism or the
Communist danger, which may have its justification, is not a pretext for
doing nothing. Change must be brought about despite these real or imagined
threats.

Ideally, a healthy nationalism is co-existent with the concept of national
sovereignty which implies the right and power to make decisions in keeping
with the nation's awareness of its own welfare. In an ideal sense, national
sovereignty can be said to exist only if all sectional interests obey the
decisions of the freely constituted authorities who speak for the nation as a
whole. Even in the most democratic state, this sovereignty is not always
achieved. In this respect the North American colonies stand out in sharp
contrast to the Spanish American portion of the continent. In the English
colonies a new nation was born as a result of the struggle for political rights
and for freedom and tolerance.[4] As Alexis de Tocqueville noted: "The social
condition of the Americans is eminently democratic; this was its character at
the foundation of the colonies and it is still more strongly marked at the
present day."[5] There is thus a positive relationship between national sovereignty and a liberal, democratic way of life. Without the usual freedoms, no

2   Eduardo Caballero Calderón, "Latinoamérica, un mundo por hacer", in *Obras* (Mede-
llin, Colombia: Bedout, 1963), p. 44.
3   Victor Alba, *Nationalists without Nations* (New York: Frederick A. Praeger, 1968), p. 16.
4   Hans Kohn, *Nationalism: Its Meaning and History*, rev. ed. (New York: Van Nostrand,
1965), p. 20.
5   Alexis de Tocqueville, *Democracy in America*. Vintage Books No.1 (New York: Knopf,
1945), p. 48.

nation can exercise that awareness which insures the perpetuation of its sovereignty.[6]

The cultural phase of nationalism has served to reinforce the political and economic aspects. It is doubtful whether any country could survive without a solid cultural base, even if economic and political needs were satisfied. What is meant by "cultural nationalism"? Historically, the cultural evolution of a people begins when the early clan or tribe manifests a number of values and circumstances held in common by its members, such as climate, territory, race, language, literature and artistic expression. The cultivation of a national spirit is of relatively recent origin, going back to the beginning of the nineteenth century, the period of romanticism; it was then that a spirit of cultural cohesion was considered essential to the existence of the State. Before then, the allegiance was pledged only to a prince or a monarch.

* * *

When the Spanish empire was fragmented in the New World, it became necessary to develop a national awareness in each of the fledgling republics by means of artistic values, figures and symbols. The rigid class structure and the consequent lack of social fluidity which characterized colonial Spanish American society constituted an obstacle to the development of a feeling of nationality in the emerging republics. Political independence had been achieved, but cultural pride and distinctiveness had not. The glorification of a national destiny had to be developed by means of literature, national holidays, military parades, martial music, patriotic orations and educational indoctrination. Furthermore, cultural nationalism assumed a variety of forms, depending upon local conditions. For example, in countries with a large indigenous and mestizo population, pre-Colombian art forms were stressed: in music, dance and clothing. These tended to supplant the Spanish element. In Mexico, for example, the Revolution of 1910 produced a veritable flowering of art forms which emphasized the autochthonous elements in painting, sculpture, music and archeology. Literature dealt with many mythological themes; even philosophy stressed the national circumstance. In Argentina the gaucho Martín Fierro was raised to the level of a national epic figure. The anti-imperialistic note has appeared frequently in the Central American novel. The indigenous element stands out in the literature of the Andean countries. Artists and writers frequently consider themselves the jealous guardians of a cultural nationalism which resists any attempt to endanger its essence and tradition.

Generally speaking, Spanish American nationalism has sought to achieve a larger degree of economic independence and, consequently, a greater

6   Salvador de Madariaga, *Essays with a Purpose* (London: Hollis & Carter, 1954), pp. 28–30.

measure of genuine political sovereignty. However, social and economic problems cannot be solved by nationalist slogans and patriotic flag-waving. Even if Latin America were to be blessed suddenly with an influx of industrial technology, it is doubtful whether all the republics of the continent would have the technical competence to realize the "great leap forward", needed to advance the economy. Foreign capital and technical assistance would still be necessary to effect a positive change in the quality of life. It is for this reason that foreign relations often make it quite impossible for nations to enjoy sovereignty in the absolute sense of the term. This is especially true of those countries which are dependent upon more powerful nations for their social and economic welfare.

The attempt to rid oneself of Spanish influence was advocated by many influential Spanish American intellectuals immediately after Independence had been achieved. Political emancipation was not enough. What was needed as well was cultural and spiritual emancipation. What many failed to see was that imitation and adoption of cultural influences, emanating from other countries, was akin to subjecting oneself once again to a form of colonialism.

For centuries the psyche of Spanish America had been buffeted by numerous forces: the picture that the Spaniard had of himself and of his nation's position in the world, the early dream of the continent as a Utopia, and the dogmas of the Catholic Church. Small wonder that the Spanish Americans, soon after Independence, began asking themselves about their social condition, their cultural circumstance, disturbed continually by such problems as national authenticity on the one hand, and dependency on the other.

For almost two hundred years Spanish America had been struggling to define its place in the world and to understand its role in history. The clash of ideas ever since Independence involved an attempt to establish a satisfactory equilibrium between political sovereignty and economic dependence, between preservation of native values and traditions, and discriminating selectivity involving acceptance in modified form or outright resistance to and rejection of foreign influences.

After the new Spanish American republics had come into being, all efforts designed to develop nationhood were beset with obstacles. At times, political struggles encountered the resistance of the Catholic Church; at others, the various countries were prevented from becoming nations because of the struggle between centralizing and federalizing tendencies. In some areas the indigenous masses were left out of the picture altogether. Without their participation, there could be no talk of nationhood.

Attempts in the political sphere to build nations were bound to fail if the basic social structures were not taken into account. Problems created by different co-existent societies had to be wrestled with and solved, such as, for example, a feudal society, rural-oriented and originating in the colonial period, an urban, merchant society, and finally, in more recent times, a capitalistic society, concerned primarily with foreign investment.[7] And always in the background, the sinister shadow of the military. The new Spanish America, in its reaction against the mother country, attempted to turn its back on the cultural values it had inherited. This was especially true of the upper classes which, in their effort to mould some sort of identity for themselves, imitated French culture patterns, a fact which was even less helpful in building an American image.

The attempt to adopt French as well as English and North American principles did not accord with Spanish American reality. Imitating the English model was not feasible. British democracy, for example, was the result of a thousand years of trial and error, of struggle and compromise, and of continual adjustment to changing circumstances. This was not the case with the emerging Spanish American republics. Needless to say, these republics were not aware of these values, not because of racial factors or because their inhabitants were temperamentally unsuited. Democratic societies are not the exclusive domain of English-speaking people.

The new republics were faced with the task of creating a feeling of nationality and constitutional government based on republican principles, unfamiliar to the great majority of the people. National sovereignty, the rights of man, and presidential elections were concepts never before experienced in Spanish America.

It is, therefore, not surprising to note, for example, a continuous change of constitutions. These could be modified or eliminated with the greatest of ease. They were not conceived of as documents formulated with great difficulty after working out a series of compromises, but rather as flamboyant proclamations of government functionaries who had come into power.

The political aspirations of the new republics may have been worthy of respect and admiration. Their constitutions, in theory, sought to insure individual freedom, common welfare and social progress. However, they never succeeded in implementing these praiseworthy objectives.

A feeling of national solidarity was difficult of realization because the continent became fragmented. Not all of the republics were able to exercise the functions of an independent nation for a variety of reasons: economic resources, the nature of the population, or the social type of organization. For example, Central America was split into five independent republics, frequently hostile to one another. A healthy nationalism could never develop as long as there were conflicts between one Spanish American country and another. Acts of hostility occurred with monotonous frequency. To a very large degree these conflicts had their origin in the lack of precise boundaries

---

[7] Victor Alba, "Nationalism and Political Reality", *America*, 18, No. 17 (1968), pp. 571–74.

between one nation and another, conditioned by economic advantage as, for example, in the case of frontier disputes between Argentina and Chile, and between Peru and Chile. In short, one may question whether an awareness of nationhood had been developed in Spanish America, whether all the inhabitants of the continent possessed the feeling that they belonged to a nation or whether they merely lived in their respective countries. It can be asserted that the social structure inherited from the colonial era still acts to keep several sub-societies from fusing into one, and thus convey to their inhabitants a feeling of being members of that larger society, i.e., a nation.

After Independence had been won, many Spanish Americans looked to Europe and the United States as models to be emulated if progress was to be achieved in the sense of expanding educational and economic opportunities, curbing reactionary tendencies wherever they might be found, and putting an end to the endless cycles of chaos followed by dictatorship.

Those who wished to shape Spanish America in the image of England, France or the United States, the so called "Europeanizers", immediately provoked a reaction in the form of the "nativists" who were interested in maintaining the old social order, with or without Spain.

The quest for ideological and organizational patterns was tied in with the attempt to describe the image of Spanish America, to modify it, or possibly, to create a new one. Thus, Sarmiento, the Argentine educator-president, seeking to destroy the "barbarism" of his country, exclaimed: "Let us be the United States of Latin America." For him Spain represented the Middle Ages and its influence had to be eliminated. Sarmiento wished to amputate the past instead of assimilating it – an understandable error committed by an impatient man. For it is important to remember: if the past is not assimilated, it is not the past. It is likely to erupt at a most unexpected moment, at times with disastrous results. Independence had been the work of the armies of the caudillos, not of the people, maintained the Chilean José Victorino Lastarria. The governing oligarchy, the privileged class, could not tolerate a feeling of solidarity and participation, to be shared in by all social classes.

Lastarria's compatriot, Francisco Bilbao, clearly preferred the democratic republic of the United States to the absolute monarchy of Spain. Perhaps an alliance with the United States would help the continent on the road to civilization. Bilbao believed that Spanish America, with its multiple territorial divisions, could not achieve nationhood until the submerged classes were recognized as an integral part of society.

The Mexican patriot, Servendo Teresa de Mier, wrote glowingly: "The North Americans, raising the flag of freedom, implanted in our hearts the names of Washington and Franklin...The United States was a new people, homogeneous, industrious, hard-working, educated and possessed of social virtues...We are an old people, heterogeneous, without any industry, allergic to work...decadent as a result of vices related to the slavery of three centuries..."[8] Francisco de Miranda, the first Spanish American to visit the United States, attributed the prosperity which he observed to the superiority of a free government over one which was despotic.[9] Sarmiento's political rival, Juan Bautista Alberdi, was also very pro-U.S. in his beliefs. "The North Americans do not sing of freedom," he wrote. "They practise it in silence. Freedom for them is not a deity, but rather an ordinary tool. Washington and his contemporaries were more interested in fighting for their individual rights and freedoms than merely for the independence of their country. Upon obtaining the former for themselves, they achieved the latter, in contrast to the countries of South America which won political independence, but not individual freedom."[10]

Yet in spite of the fact that the United States was held up as a model to be imitated, that country did very little to promote the concept of freedom outside its geographical boundaries. Bolívar himself was chagrined: "The United States seems destined by Providence to plague America with misery in the name of liberty."[11]

The tragedy of Spanish America, then, was the result of attempts to apply to the new republics political norms and ideas which had been developed in other countries, but which had nothing to do with the experience or conditions of these republics.

Spanish American "Europeanizers" thought that if the continent would emulate the best of the Old World, it would improve its well being. But there was another side to the coin. Europe, and subsequently the United States, were indeed interested in being imitated, but giving to Latin America only that which accorded with their interests. The result was negative: Latin American dependence and marginality. Latin America had tried to join the Western family of nations. To this end it had welcomed European doctrines, such as liberalism and positivism. Perhaps, it was thought, these infusions of culture could aid in the development of the continent and help it find itself. On the other hand, if these were found wanting, the continent would do well in seeking inspiration and guidance in the native landscape and the heritage of the indigenous peoples in order to define more clearly its American identity. Surely the vigorous qualities of Spanish America's natural resources, as well as the vital tradition of pre-Colombian society, could be an effective antidote to the social and economic ills inherited from Western civilization. Such was the expected reaction of the nativists or "Americanists", as opposed to the "Europeanizers".

8 Quoted in Carlos M. Rama, *La imagen de los Estados Unidos en la América Latina* (México: Sep Diana, 1975), pp. 55–56.

9 Carlos Rangel, *Del buen salvaje al buen revolucionario* (Caracas: Monte Avila, 1976), p. 40.

10 Quoted in Carlos M. Rama, p. 68.

11 Leopoldo Zea, *Latin American and the World*. Translated by F. K. Hendricks and B. Berler (Norman, Okla.: University of Oklahoma Press, 1969), pp. 55–56.

All arguments and counter-arguments relative to the essence or desired image of Spanish America were intimately related to the way in which the continent perceived itself vis-à-vis the United States, Europe and, more recently, the rest of the world. In some quarters imitation of foreign models was considered anathema to authentic cultural identity. Yet the very concept is a dynamic one. Cultural identity or national image, in short, a picture which one has of oneself, has continued to evolve in time and space. It is no longer a question of whether to imitate or not to imitate. It depends on what it is that one wishes to imitate. Imitation in and of itself can be good or bad. It should not be posited in opposition to originality or authenticity of culture, Spanish American or otherwise. What is original? Authentic? The definition depends on the person or group that attempts it; its position in society, its ideology and interests.

In short, originality should not be sought after as an end in itself. What is original can be the manner in which one imitates or adopts and utilizes. As the Bolivian philosopher, Guillermo Francovich, has put it: "He who attempts to be original ends up being eccentric."[12] No one is suggesting that Spanish America cut itself off from universal culture of which it is an integral part, and to forge an "original" culture – obviously an impossibility. What the Spanish American can do, however, is to select elements from the vast storehouse and adapt them to his circumstances; to live universal culture in a Spanish American manner. This process will constitute his originality. The roots will be American; one does not adopt Old-World style as though it were a suit of clothes to be put on. Once this attitude is assumed, the hairsplitting concerning cultural identity will find itself operating in a vacuum, to be replaced by another, perhaps more relevant set of questions. The problem of identity will no longer be seen as one, monolithic whole. Instead, we will be faced with multiple identities even in the same person. As far as the term "America" is concerned, it is obvious that geographic, historical, and ethnic factors serve to introduce frustrating variables which impede the formulation of a satisfactory definition. Furthermore, in attempting to arrive at a valid and satisfactory definition and appreciation of Spanish American identity, the Scylla and Charybdis syndrome has to be avoided, namely, picturing the Spanish American socio-political scene as a pale imitation of European culture or a scenario without any European roots whatsoever. Needless to say, Spanish American cultural essence is neither wholly European nor Indian. Observable culture patterns partake of both sources. This last point requires further clarification, especially because of its linkage to the concept of tradition, a term which generally emerges in any discussion of national identity.

* * *

---

[12] Guillermo Francovich, "Pachamama", in *Antología de Filosofía Americana Contemporánea*, ed. Leopoldo Zea (México, D.F.: B. Costa-Amic, 1968), p. 87.

Traditional values, like nationalism or patriotism, can be utilized as a weapon to further the interests of specific groups in society. For example, those who would identify Spanish American traditions with Spanish Catholicism forget that many leaders in the movement for Independence were "free thinkers" and Masons. Tradition is thus a pluralistic concept. No one group exercises an exclusive monopoly over its utilization. Moreover, one would do well to distinguish between tradition and traditionalism. The former embodies the basic values and moral codes which govern the behavior of a people. Tradition, in a dynamic sense, contains elements which can be applied to changing circumstances. On the other hand, traditionalism best describes a set of concepts which can be said to be frozen in time. Its precepts are rigid and considered eternal. Customs become moral norms and tend to oppose progressive adaptation to novel conditions.

Yet not all conservatives are necessarily traditionalists. The Spanish Catholic philosopher Manuel García Morente, although politically conservative, shares the notion of a dynamic concept of tradition. Tradition is not inflexible, he maintains, nor is it reactionary. "It does not represent hostility to progress; on the contrary, it holds that national progress should be implemented...in accordance with the style which defines the essence of nationality."[13] Again, one may well ask in this connection: What is the essence of nationality? Is Spanish nationality progressive or conservative? Which elements predominate? Is the nationalism of traditionalism equivalent to that of tradition? How much room is allowed for critical-mindedness and dissent? The positive and negative aspects of nationalism are illustrated by the fact that the nationalism of a disadvantaged country can be a force for a progressive movement in history, whereas that of a dominant nation which seeks to expand its power and influence can utilize nationalist sentiment to arouse enmity against those whom it seeks to dominate. The distinctive aspect of Spanish American nationalism can be said to be positive when it opposes colonialism or imperialism. However, that self-same nationalism will lose its progressive character if it is utilized for military adventure and suppression of hard-won democratic rights.

[13] Manuel García Morente, *Idea de la hispanidad* (Madrid: Espasa-Calpe, 1961), pp. 53–54.

6

A VIEW OF SPANISH AMERICA

Reactions to and evaluations of the American fact continued unabated. Attitudes which crystallized into critical comment came from several directions. Europeans became Americans, and Americans became North and South Americans, Anglo-and-Spanish Americans, conditioned by circumstances, background and heritage, and by the social and economic ideologies of the respective mother countries.

The two Americas had this much in common: they both began as colonies. Thereafter their paths diverged radically. The United States, with its emphasis on individual initiative, private enterprise, Calvinistic work ethic and liberal political philosophy, embarked upon a policy of territorial and economic expansion until it assumed a position of power and status in the international arena. By contrast, the Disunited States of Spanish America were preoccupied with attempts to put their house in order, swept up as they were by chaos, military rule and an inability to leave their imprint upon world markets. Spanish America had been left behind; all the choice seats were being occupied rapidly by others in the economic theatre. Twentieth-century evaluation and criticism intensified. Alfonso Reyes, the Mexican thinker, wrote: "We arrived late at the banquet of European civilization." The Peruvian José Carlos Mariátegui had expressed the same idea in Marxist terms: "The age of free competition in the capitalist economy is at an end...We have entered the stage of monopolies, of empires. The Latin American countries have been late in arriving at the scene of capitalist competition...The destiny of our countries within the capitalist order is that of simple colonies."[1]

And so quite a few Spanish Americans looked at themselves and at the United States, and did not like what they saw. For example, the Argentine sociologist Carlos Octavio Bunge studied the racial mix found in many Spanish American countries. His comments were blatantly racist, stressing as they did the negative characteristics of the continent's inhabitants. "The Spaniards," he wrote, "gave us arrogance, laziness, theological uniformity;

[1] Roberto Fernández Retamar, *Calibán cannibale* (Paris: François Maspero, 1973), p. 118.

48

the Indian, fatalism and ferocity, the negroes, servility...,"[2] all of which, according to Bunge, made for the progressive degeneration of the so-called Latin American.

The Bolivian Alcides Arguedas, in his *Pueblo enfermo*,[3] manifested open hostility toward his "sick country", because its population was predominantly Indian and mestizo. For him, the Indian was submissive and resigned. The mestizo was lazy and given to drink if he was a member of the lower classes, and a master of duplicity, fabrication and intrigue if he occupied a higher position on the social ladder.

On the other hand, José Martí, the "Apostle of Cuba", adopted a firm position against racism of any kind. There is no race hatred, he asserted, because there aren't any races.[4] The racist concept causes confusion, he stated. A man is more than merely white, mulatto or black. Blacks, as well as whites, are divided according to their qualities; they can be timid or valiant, self-effacing or selfish. Insisting on racial differences, he concluded, is an obstacle to individual and public welfare.

In the period which followed the Wars of Independence, Spanish America found itself buffeted by two opposing ideological currents. One emphasized the desirability of continuing in the tradition of the mother country and perpetuating the cultural attitudes of Spain; the other stressed the need for a complete break, not only political, but also spiritual. The newly-formed republics had to be guided along the lines of a democratic philosophy and led out of the retarding influences of a colonial heritage.

The Argentine romantic, Esteban Echeverría, had declaimed against the backward nature of the society inherited from the mother country. Spanish America had to break with this past, he insisted. "America must learn the lesson that infallible authority should be replaced by the unfettered play of ideas."[5] "We have achieved political independence," lamented Echeverría, "but culturally and spiritually we are still dependent upon Spain."[6] The complaint was echoed repeatedly. "We are Europeans, born in America," stated his compatriot, Juan Bautista Alberdi.[7] American culture was merely a branch of the European tree. The American, as an offspring of a European mother, was possessed of a feeling of dependency. America's essential being thus remained undefined, if not entirely concealed.

---

2   Luis Alberto Sánchez, *Examen espectral de América Latina*, 2nd ed. (Buenos Aires: Editorial Losada, 1962), pp. 116–17.

3   Alcides Arguedas, *Pueblo enfermo*, 3rd ed. (La Paz: Ediciones Puerta del Sol, 1936).

4   José Martí, "Nuestra América", in Carlos Ripoll, *Conciencia intelectual de América* (New York: Las Américas, 1966), p. 231.

5   Esteban Echeverría, *Dogma Socialista* (La Plata: 1940), pp. 145–46.

6   Echeverría, p. 187.

7   Juan Bautista Alberdi, "*Bases...*", in *Antología del pensamiento social y político de América Latina*, edited by Leopoldo Zea and Abelardo Villegas (Washington, D.C.: Unión Panamericana, 1964), p. 285.

The anti-Spanish stance was countered by the foremost representative of the opposing school of thought. Andrés Bello can perhaps be said to have come more closely than anyone else in Latin America to the Renaissance concept of the "universal man". Bello aligned himself with that group of Spanish American intellectuals which endeavored to preserve the positive aspects of Spain's cultural heritage.

Bello did not advance any exaggerated claims for Spain's record in the New World. He was as much opposed to the "black legend",[8] the one-sided indictment of Spain's mismanagement of the colonies, as he was to the "white legend", an attempt to whitewash the Spanish record. Bello wished to synthesize the best of the Hispanic tradition with the optimum potential of the new American environment. The new republics, he maintained, should never be a pale imitation of Europe. One must assimilate the best of what Europe had to offer, but not in order to imitate it in servile fashion. Instead, the new republics should discuss, apply and modify to suit the native environment. Only in this way could the New World culture acquire an American imprint and avoid the cultivation of "exotic" plants.

Bello's moderate stance, his avoidance of political extremes, did not prevent him from giving enthusiastic support to a plan which called for the convening of an American Confederation. Under the terms of this project each nation would maintain its autonomy; the Confederation, as such, would be prohibited from interfering in the internal affairs of any of its constituent members. Bello speaks of this proposal as an extension of Bolívar's original dream, a beautiful utopia in its day, but now, ten years later, "we are of a different opinion".[9]

The countries of Spanish America, he goes on to say, have been separated far too long; their interests, their language and cultural heritage, should bring them closer together. What is noteworthy in this connection is the complete absence in Bello's thinking of any anti-Yankee reference. On the contrary, he does not exclude the United States from possible participation in the proposed confederation which may conceivably serve as a counterweight to the political activities of European alliances. Let us not forget, he hastens to add, that the independence of the North American colonies is complementary to ours. Bello refers to the United States as "the great Republic of the North, a model of wisdom and sanity".[10] Appealing to his compatriots, he exclaims:

---

[8]   The "black legend" perpetuates the accusation that Spaniards were wicked and cruel in their behavior toward the Indians. It should be pointed out that the British, Dutch and French behaved equally badly in the colonial period. Conquerors are unwelcome anywhere; the Spaniards were no exception. "Spain did not introduce cruelty and war; exploitation was an old story to the Indians." (Hubert Herring, *A History of Latin America – From the Beginnings to the Present*, 2nd rev. ed. [New York: Alfred A. Knopf, 1961] p. 153).

[9]   Andrés Bello, "La Confederación de Hispanoamérica", in *Bello*, ed. Gabriel Méndez Plancarte (México: Ediciones de la Secretaría de Educación Pública, 1943), p. 84.

[10] Bello, p. 88.

"If we continue to present to the world the scandal provoked by our ambitious aspirations and rebellions, if we continue to babble all sorts of theories, while deficient in trade, arts, schools; in short, if we are seen as being at a standstill, or even moving backward in the march towards civilization and industrial prosperity, as occurs in the majority of our republics... then we shall discredit the republican institutions, we shall becloud the brilliance bequeathed unto them by the outstanding achievements of the Washingtons and Franklins..."[11]

In our own day the antithetical positions are given additional emphasis by two Mexican thinkers. According to the historian Edmundo O'Gorman, America would like to be like Europe in order to be itself. Not so, retorts, O'Gorman's compatriot, the philosopher Leopoldo Zea: "America would like to have what Europe possesses in order to develop, but not be a copy of Europe."[12]

It is important to remember in this connection that what is "native" is not necessarily "inferior" to that which is European. It is always possible that a given characteristic or solution to a problem may be "foreign" today, but will in time become part of the cultural identity in the course of the developmental process. And yet, contemporary thinkers continue their quest of the "essence" of Spanish America, seeking to define what is authentic and original in its configuration, and to discover its component elements. This very fact, it seems, is indicative of a feeling of uneasiness, of dissatisfaction with one's being, and of a desire to assert one's identity. But identity in what sense? Up to what point do Americans still have one foot in the Old World ? How much is "new" in the New World?

The idea of America, then, presented an unenviable challenge to thinkers and writers – beginning with Simón Bolívar – to explain to themselves and to the world, the nature of the continent. Many of them attempted to put flesh upon the skeleton, casting about for models which would serve to inspire and influence the course of its future development. The United States inspired some and disappointed others as the decades passed and historical circumstances played out their drama. At first the United States was admired for the freedom it accorded its citizens and for its equality of opportunity. Subsequently, when it embarked upon its policy of expansionism, it provoked fear, resentment and antagonism.

Political independence was not enough. It was necessary to create and develop an authentically American awareness and free the former colonies from Spanish influences. Although many Spanish Americans had looked upon the United States as a model, even before Independence was won, Bolívar thought that blind imitation of that country would not solve the problems of

---

11 Bello, p. 88.
12 Abelardo Villegas, *La filosofía de lo mexicano* (México: Fondo de Cultura Económica, 1960), p. 204.

the Latin American continent. As a matter of fact, the United States itself was ambivalent with respect to the Spanish American War of Independence for purely economic reasons. It was afraid of the potential competition which would be offered by England; the latter favored independence for the Spanish colonies since it was commercially advantageous. The United States attitude was clearly expressed by John Adams: "England would gain the most in such a turn of affairs...and England, unfortunately, we cannot trust."[13]

Additional negative commentary which issued forth from the United States came from none other than Thomas Jefferson. He had his doubts about the new republics to the south, and expressed them unequivocally: "I wish I could give better hopes to our southern brothers," he wrote. "The achievement of their independence of Spain is no longer a question. But it is a very serious one. What will become of them? Ignorance and bigotry...are incapable of self-government. They will fall under military despotism and become the murderous tools of their respective Bonapartes."[14]

Another instance of U.S. negative attitudes at the time of Bolívar is quoted by Lewis Hanke from the unsigned review of a work on history, appearing in the *North American Review*: "We have no concern with South America...we can have no well-founded political sympathy with them. We are sprung from different stock, we speak different languages, we have been brought up in different social and moral schools, we have been governed by different codes of laws, we profess radically different forms of religion..."[15]

And this, despite the fact that Jefferson, as well as Washington and Franklin, were admired by the "southern brothers".

In his famous "Jamaica Letter", written on September 6, 1815, Bolívar had expressed the hope of seeing America develop into the greatest nation in the world by virtue of her freedom and glory. However, he was realistic enough to realize that the New World would not, at least in his time, be consolidated into a single nation, united by a single bond. Although it is reasonable to suppose, he went on to say, that since the various parts of Spanish America have a common origin, language, customs and religion, they ought to have a single government to allow the newly formed states to unite in a confederation. However, this was not possible. The continent was "separated by climatic differences, geographic diversity, conflicting interests and dissimilar characteristics".[16]

---

[13] José de Onís, *The United States as Seen by Spanish American Writers* (New York: Gordian Press, 1975), p. 23.

[14] R. L. Bruckberger, *Image of America*. Translated from the French by C. G. Paulding and Virgilio Peterson (New York: The Viking Press, 1959), p. 75.

[15] Lewis Hanke, *Do The Americans Have a Common History?* (New York: Alfred A. Knopf, 1964), p. 5.

[16] Simón Bolívar, *His Basic Thoughts*, ed. Manuel Pérez Vila (Caracas: Academia Nacional de la Historia, 1980), p. 78.

The Jamaica letter also afforded Bolívar the opportunity to review the past and present, and speculate on the future of the continent. It was on this occasion, too, that he expressed the fervent wish to convene an assembly in Panama, attended by representatives of all the nations of the Continent, for the purpose of deliberating upon questions of peace in the world: "This type of organization," he wrote, "may come to pass in some happier period of our regeneration."[17]

Bolívar was quite disappointed. He has expected more from Europe and the United States in the War of Independence. "How unfortunate were our expectations," wrote the Great Liberator. "Not only the Europeans, but our brothers from the north have remained simple spectators of the struggle."[18] Bolívar was aware of the differences between the two Americas, yet he believed that Spanish America could learn a good deal from the United States.

In his address to the Congress of Venezuela in 1819, he speaks admiringly of the U.S. Constitution. It is a miracle, he observes, that a federal Constitution has existed in North America to such a successful degree. The people of the United States represent an unusual example of "political virtue and moral rectitude".[19] The inhabitants of North America are "unique in the history of the human race"[20] for having been able to preserve the federal system of government despite the difficult circumstances which have prevailed.

* * *

Despite the fact that one may wish to avoid the ever-present danger of stereotyping the inhabitants of the two Americas, it must nevertheless be admitted that certain characteristics and behavior patterns may be evident in a significant number of members of a socio-cultural or national group. Of course, the term "significant" is open to question. Although these traits or qualities may be considered as "typical", it is always difficult to assert with certainty that they are to be found in the majority of that group's population. Yet it cannot be denied that these patterns of behavior have been influential in imprinting a definite stamp on the cultural contours of a given country and in moulding its institutions.

The attempt to define what is "typically" American, or specifically, to try to answer the question: "Who or what is an American?" is fraught with difficulties, not to mention obstacles and pitfalls of all sorts. To factor out all the items (qualities, characteristics, values and attitudes) commonly assumed

17 Bolívar, p. 79.
18 Onís, p. 24.
19 Bolívar at the Congress of Venezuela, February 13, 1819. Translated by J. Hamilton (Caracas, 1974), p. 7.
20 Bolívar, Congress of Venezuela, p. 7.

to comprise the cluster of elements that describe the American (North or South) is a frustrating process. One discovers, for example, that the ingredients which are supposedly shared by the vast majority of the inhabitants of the United States are not as numerous, and that those which remain in an effort to establish some measure of commonality, are not necessarily or uniquely "American". The four freedoms (assembly, religion, expression, press) which are basic to the concept of the North American creed may well be claimed by some countries of Western Europe as well.

Any attempt to compare the Spanish American with the citizen of the United States may well be an exercise in futility, or as Bolívar would have it, "to plow the sea". The obstacles in the way of arriving at some sort of acceptable characterization of a national or continental "type" are endless. The variables are numerous and resist classification. If one were to try to establish some sort of cultural image or recognizable identity, one would have to wrestle with stereotypes, prejudices and popular misconceptions. The picture which generally emerges is the result of personal contact, emotional reactions and psychological mechanisms – all of which, taken together, cannot be depended upon to yield a valid, composite portrait, representative of the majority of a given group. At best, it would represent a small minority.

Latin America is not a unitary entity, geographically, racially and culturally. Geographically, the continent is characterized by extreme topographical variations. The mountainous areas, coastal regions, plains, forests and deserts, exert their influence upon the inhabitants who, in turn, reveal a considerable degree of heterogeneity in their attitudes, value systems and behavior patterns. Is the "Indian" population itself homogeneous? Not at all. There are numerous variations among the aboriginal peoples, not to mention the fact that they speak more than a thousand different languages.[21]

Aside from the obvious fact that there are vast geographical differences within the continent, the difficulty partakes of linguistic and racial aspects as well. The majority of Latin Americans descend from Iberians, Indians and Blacks. The term "Iberian" presents the first complication: Iberians are Spaniards and Portuguese. Spaniards are Castilians, Andalusians, Catalans and Basques. To this is added the temporal factor which introduces a dynamic note into the cultural picture. For example, the Castilian of today is not the same as his countryman of three or four centuries ago. As far as the "Indian" is concerned, there is no ethnic "type" either. The Mayas were as different from the Incas as the English are from the Arabs. The cultural life of the native inhabitants varied from the most highly-developed civilizations to the lifestyle of the most elementary nomadic tribes.

And what of the Blacks? An examination of their African origins will

---

[21] J. M. Briceño Guerrero, "Unidad y diversidad de Latino-américa", *Anuario, Latino América*, México, UNAM, 2 (1969), p. 164.

reveal that there is an equal degree of heterogeneity, characteristic of the various groups that were brought over as slaves to the New World. How, then, can one speak of the cultural identity of the Spanish American? The picture becomes even more complicated if we add to the original population (including the Portuguese), immigrant groups which arrived subsequently from Europe and Asia. What results, then, is a picture of diversity and heterogeneity, the only terms to which we can apply the designation "typical".

On a popular level of discourse it is far too easy to engage in the use of stereotyped judgments when one attempts to study so-called characteristics of the American - North and South. Snap judgments still abound, at times in over-simplified form, at others in more subtle fashion and on a more sophisticated level. For example, the Mexican philosopher, José Vasconcelos, maintained that "the Yankee is hardworking, has stick-to-itiveness; Latin Americans are inconstant and indolent, but have a clear superiority in mental quickness".[22]

Vasconcelos's compatriot, Leopoldo Zea, believes that the Spanish American stresses spiritual culture, whereas the North American places greater emphasis upon material values and technology. In an attempt to further refine the contrast, Zea labels the man from the North a "practical idealist" (idealista práctico) in the sense that he is more concerned with the reality within which his ideas are implemented and modified, if need be. On the other hand, the Spanish American is an "idealistic practitioner" (práctico idealista) who attempts to impose his ideas upon a resistant and stubborn reality. Furthermore, the nature of the projects in which each group is involved serves to emphasize the differences between them. The two attitudes complement each other and may conceivably blend into a harmonious synthesis.[23]

One would hesitate to explain an individual's behavior on the basis of his nationality or ethnicity. A description of national character in this connection would probably amount to an enumeration of tendencies when considering different cultural groups. For example, Americans in the United States are considered to be "joiners", more so than citizens of other nations. The situation is further complicated by the fact that concepts, definitions and attitudes are dynamic, and are continually undergoing change.

Is the "Ugly American", for example, "typical" of the U.S. citizen? Or is he representative of a very restrictive sampling of a socio-economic group? One is forced to conclude that the so-called "typical" case or stereotype is "typical" only of an insignificant minority of a given group.

---

[22] Quoted by William Rex Crawford, *A Century of Latin American Thought* (Cambridge, MA.: Harvard University Press, 1945), p. 265.

[23] Leopoldo Zea, *América como conciencia* (México: Ediciones Cuadernos Americanos, 1953), p. 145.

Quite a few Spanish American authors have described the "characteristics" of their respective countrymen. In most of these cases, these are
fleeting impressions based on subjective and superficial reactions. For
example, the Chilean Benjamín Subercasseaux describes his compatriot as
unstable and irresponsible, but capable of an extreme degree of efficiency if
the task at hand appeals to him.[24] Interestingly enough, there is often marked
disagreement among the analysts themselves. Subercasseaux maintains that
the "roto", the so-called man of the people, is a completely disoriented
personality without any stable beliefs or ideals, whereas Hernán San Martín
considers the "roto" to be representative of the Chilean nation, and presents
him as an essential ingredient of national pride and dignity.[25]

It should be remembered that Chile consists of people who have migrated
from various countries of the world. These diverse nationalities brought with
them different virtues and defects. One might well ask to what extent the
Chilean environment has contributed to the moulding of these disparate
groups into a supposedly homogeneous cultural entity. One may also venture
the suggestion that lists of virtues and defects tend to acquire a more stable
character in simple, unsophisticated communities. These traits probably tend
to be of longer duration and consistency than is the case in modern, urban
societies where they undergo more rapid change.

The fact remains that Spanish American "traits" or "personality" cannot
be defined solely in terms of ethnic characteristics, simply because ethnicity
is so varied. The only Spanish American "essence" or "nature" one can
speak of and still maintain a valid point of view would be couched in terms
of common problems which confront the various segments of the population.

Ethnic multiplicity becomes apparent as one proceeds from one area of
Spanish America to another. For example, in Colombia, the hybridization of
white and Indian is totally different from that of Argentina where European
immigrants mixed with the native population. Mexico and Guatemala are
quite different, racially, from Costa Rica and Uruguay. In Peru and Bolivia a
white minority exists in a sea of indigenous elements. Furthermore, the black
inhabitants in certain regions, not to mention the Chinese, have also caused
racial transformations of a different sort. Latin America possesses all the
necessary ingredients for the formation of José Vasconcelos's "cosmic
race". There is room for a certain degree of optimism, as manifested by the
Colombian Caballero Calderón, who echoes Vasconcelos's dream of a cosmic race, the product of all races whose mind would be open to all truths.[26]

[24] Javier Pinedo, "La ensayística y el problema de la identidad, 1960–1988", in *Los
Ensayistas*, ed. J. L. Gómez Mártinez and F. J. Pinedo (Athens, Georgia: University of Georgia,
1987–88), p. 232.
[25] Pinedo, p. 242.
[26] Eduardo Caballero Calderón, *Obras* (Medellín, Colombia: Bedout, 1963), p. 20. In later

Let us consider still another case of national "characteristics", namely that of Costa Rica. In an attempt to analyze the personality of the Costa Rican, we cannot ignore geographical and historical influences. Furthermore, as has been pointed out, there is probably a difference between the urban dweller and the inhabitants of rural communities. However, at this point, another difficulty must be pointed out: it is difficult to establish the parameters of each. Even though we have thus far been loath to posit the existence of common cultural traits because of our desire to avoid generalities and stereotypes, it has nevertheless been conceded by psychologists and sociologists, however reluctantly, that certain common traits may exist in a country, in both urban and rural areas, although there are variations in degree.[27] Although one may choose to disagree, an outstanding personality trait of the Costa Rican, according to Rodríguez Vega, is his timidity and excessive shyness, attributed to centuries-old isolation in rural areas, dating back to the colonial period. In spite of the fact that villages have become towns, and towns have developed into cities, the urban dweller still retains vestiges of extreme reserve in his human relationships. Unfortunately, there is a negative aspect to this characteristic, namely, distrust and suspicion, more pronounced in the rural dweller, due to lack of social contact.[28]

This judgment brings to mind a point of view expressed by the Argentine Ezequiel Martínez Estrada, who also argues that geography plays a dominant role in the formation of character traits. The vast stretches of sparsely inhabited territory, especially the Argentine pampas, are conducive to isolation and solitude. Lack of communication results in superficial contacts and absence of lasting friendships. Solitude serves to develop timidity and suspicion. The inhabitants of the Pampas are lacking in generosity; they are spiritually impoverished because "solitude is poverty".[29] "They wish to enjoy themselves but they don't know how. They want to love and are grotesque..."[30]

Are there personality attributes which can be said to differentiate a group of Spanish Americans that belong to one country from those who are natives of another? Rodríguez Vega believes that the Costa Rican is different from the Cuban or the Argentine. He maintains that the concept of nationality is not too crystallized in the case of Costa Rica and that, therefore, the Costa Rican does not experience the feeling of nationalism, so easily evoked in the

---

years Vasconcelos, in a more pessimistic vein, confessed to this author that his book, *La raza cósmica*, was just another instance of the follies of youth.

27 Eugenio Rodríguez Vega, "Debe y haber del hombre costarricense", *Revista de la Universidad de Costa Rica*, No. 10 (1954), pp. 9–32.

28 Eugenio Rodríguez Vega, *Apuntes para una sociología costarricense* (San José: Edición Universitaria 1953), pp. 28–30.

29 Ezequiel Martínez Estrada, *Radiografía de la pampa*, 5th ed. (Buenos Aires: Losada, 1953), p. 116.

30 Martínez Estrada, p. 115.

others. This is because he is lacking in historical tradition which so often provides the motive force behind the fomenting of patriotic emotions.[31] However, one may add sceptically that the Costa Rican, not unlike other Spanish Americans, is sure to experience a feeling of patriotism in times of national crisis, a feeling which can be just as strong as that which can be found elsewhere on the continent. Once the crisis is past, the awareness of nationality recedes.

On the positive side, one may say that the Costa Rican's predilection for democratic values has been conditioned by historical factors. For example, the country never experienced the rule of strong men who imposed their will upon the people. Scant in population and without an indigenous labor force, it never offered propitious conditions for the development of privileged castes.

Students of the Costa Rican character have pointed to the "choteo" – i.e., the mocking spirit manifested toward one's fellows – as a negative trait. The "choteo", also found in Cuba, occurs at all levels of society and has been explained psychologically as an attempt to compensate for one's timidity. It can vary from friendly, gentle irony to more vitriolic barbs. The Costa Rican who occasionally ventures to exhibit extrovert tendencies in a social situation becomes the object of sarcastic comments, since he has, apparently, violated a well-established culture pattern.[32]

Argentina is an outstanding example of a Spanish American nation which engages in self-analysis and criticism as manifested in the works of many of its essayists and novelists. For example, Eduardo Mallea demonstrates a considerable measure of anguish as he performs psychological surgery on his nation's inhabitants. Argentina exasperates him. There are in reality two Argentinas, he claims: one which is "visible", driven by ambition, corruption and material values of the city, and the other "invisible" sector which is concentrated in the healthier environment of the countryside, where the people are pure, honest and sensitive. It is this latter segment of Argentine society that should become "visible", since it constitutes the hope of the nation.[33]

In another essay, *La vida blanca*, Mallea continues in a similar vein. An individual, he complains, is judged in his country by the amount of power he can exert, and not by the intrinsic qualities of his being. What he has is more important than what he is.[34] This accounts for the scepticism and demoralization of Argentine youth.

The Argentine philosopher Victor Massuh also criticizes his countrymen: Argentines, he states, suffer from a lack of memory. They have no sense of

[31] Rodríguez Vega, "Debe y haber...", p. 29.
[32] Rodríguez Vega, *Apuntes...*, p. 32.
[33] Eduardo Mallea, *Historia de una pasión argentina*, 6th ed. (Madrid: Espasa-Calpe, 1969), Ch. 3, 4.

history, no notion of the process of continuity, which means that they are always beginning something, living from day to day, in an eternal present. This also implies that they are constantly repeating, starting at point zero, without ever trying a new approach. Moreover, Massuh continues, the role of intelligence in Argentina has given way to clever astuteness. Intelligence is utilized when one faces problems in order to solve them; astuteness serves the function of eluding these problems and merely gives the *impression* of having solved them.[35]

The Argentine is at his best when acting as an individual, but as a member of a group he appears in a most unfavorable light. In the latter instance, responsibility gives way to irresponsibility, quality is replaced by quantity, and creativity yields to mediocrity.[36] This devastating criticism is illustrative of the fact that Spanish Americans can also indulge in stereotyped judgments when criticising themselves as well as others.

In an interview with the journalist Bernardo Neustadt, Alejandro Orfila, former secretary of the Organization of American States, asserts that Argentines have an inferiority complex; they are always on the defensive.[37] By contrast, the North American is not afraid of self-criticism. The latter has a sense of teamwork; he knows what he wants and achieves a maximum result with a minimum of effort.[38] In the United States success is looked upon favorably. Regrettably, this is not the case in Argentina.

Rootlessness is a basic characteristic of Argentine life, according to the Argentine essayist, Julio Mafud. Significant sectors of Argentine society have always been separated from one another. The wave of European immigration has overwhelmed the older "native" lifestyle, and the subsequent, at times forced, amalgamation has resulted in social conflict and psychological anxieties.[39]

This pessimistic analysis is shared by Mafud's countryman, the sociologist Norberto Rodríguez Bustamante, who examines the Argentine personality, and finds that the outstanding traits are: a feeling of permanent discontent, an air of suspicion and scepticism, a lack of confidence, and a sense of alienation, as these relate to the social, economic and political components of society. In short, Rodríguez Bustamante is witness to what he believes is the degenerative process of the Argentine personality, one which

34 Eduardo Mallea, *La vida blanca* (Buenos Aires: Sur, 1960), p. 134.

35 Bernardo Neustadt, *La Argentina y los argentinos* (Buenos Aires: Emecé 1976), pp. 241–42.

36 Neustadt, p. 244.

37 Neustadt, p. 276.

38 Neustadt, p. 277.

39 *Historia de la literatura argentina*, 3, *Los Contemporáneos* (Buenos Aires: Centro Editor de América Latina, 1968), p. 1278.

is steeped in confusion, ignorance and blindness with respect to possibilities for the future.[40]

The renowned Argentine novelist-essayist, Ernesto Sábato, also reflects upon the "authentic" character of his countrymen. Taking the year 1930 as his point of departure, the year which marks the shattering economic and political crisis of the nation, Sábato contends that many Argentines believe that there is no such entity as national "authenticity". The vast diversity, characteristic of the population, militates against the formation of "typical" traits. In fact, it is preferable to be diverse and multifaceted, rather than limited and uniform.[41] Referring to literary creativity, Sábato admits that there are suggestions of a "national" literature, at least beginning with Sarmiento and the gaucho poetry of José Hernández. Yet many more novels are needed, much more remains to be written in order to arrive at a true picture of the contradictory Argentine reality. There is no absolute "originality" or "authenticity". Everything rests on what has gone on before. It is impossible, he concludes, to find "purity" in anything created by humans. Every culture is hybrid.

The emphasis on the negative is demonstrated once more by H. A. Murena, a foremost disciple of Ezequiel Martínez Estrada. Extending his canvas from his native Argentina to the continent as a whole, he attempts a psychoanalytic approach to his depiction of the Spanish American personality. Spanish Americans, he claims, are the dispossessed of the world. They have foresaken history; they did so when they left Europe. The resultant feeling of anguish has given rise to fear which, in the Argentine, is manifested as silence and lack of communication, as well as fear of illness and death. Two contradictory attitudes, both equally bad, result from this syndrome: one is the shutting out of Argentine reality and substituting a permanent nostalgia for Europe; the other, a rejection of Europe and its culture. The tragedy lies in an inability to synthesize native values with universalism. Murena holds that the problem will be solved when Argentina severs the umbilical cord which binds it to Spain, and thus eliminates the conflicts in which the country is immersed. Only then will it be able to flourish culturally.

The problem is essentially bio-psychological. It is akin to the conflict between the child and its parents, i.e., the experience and cultural history of the parents become obstacles in the spiritual development of the child. Only after cutting the bonds which unite Argentina with the country of its origin, and thus achieving cultural independence, will Argentina be in a position to effect a rapprochement with Spain (if it chooses to) and realize a higher synthesis. Failure to do so has caused Argentine historians with liberal,

[40] Ibid., p. 1288.
[41] Ernesto Sábato, *La cultura en la encrucijada nacional* (Buenos Aires: Editorial Sudamericana, 1976), p. 17.

democratic and Europe-oriented tendencies to clash continually with historians who are inclined to adhere to a nativist, anti-European and caudillo tendency. These conflicts have been, at least in part, responsible for the perpetual national crises.

Mexico, too, has been "analyzed" and presents an outstanding example of how Spanish Americans perceive themselves. The search for national identity in this case can perhaps be said to have begun after the Mexican Revolution. Attempts to define the Mexican personality were undeniably influenced by the writings of Ortega y Gasset. Samuel Ramos, utilizing Ortega's doctrine of perspectivism, analyzed the Mexican in terms of the historical influences to which the country had been subjected. Mexico suffers from a feeling of inferiority which had its origin in the period of conquest and colonization. The war with the United States had not helped much either. Ramos, making use of Adlerian psychology, advances the hypothesis that the Mexican is lacking in self-confidence. He is constantly on the defensive and belligerant in order to bolster his ego. He must feel that others are always inferior, he is irritable and incapable of self-criticism. Nevertheless, Ramos feels that he must offer a word of comfort: the Mexican is really not inferior; he merely thinks he is.[42]

Many other studies dot the Mexican scene: data taken not only from the field of psychology, but from sociology and philosophy as well.[43] Some studies are more controlled experimentally than others. Octavio Paz is more poetic, maintaining for example, that the Mexican woman's inferiority is constitutional. "In surrendering, they open up...their wound never heals...Every opening of the male being involves a diminution of manliness".[44] Manliness is never supposed to break down; to confide is a sign of weakness. This "machismo", it should be remembered, is not necessarily confined to Mexico.

In connection with the discussion of cultural identity, the Venezuelan philosopher Ernesto Mays Vallenilla, offers some interesting, although debatable, insights into the Spanish American personality. He challenges the American credo as the land of hope in the future. Hope is not the quality to be stressed. Instead, expectancy is the characteristic trait, and the two should not be confused. According to Mays Vallenilla, that which characterizes the Spanish American is his continuous air of expectancy. He is always waiting for something to happen; he expects it to happen and anticipates its impending appearance. What is about to occur does not have to be good or bad; this in itself would serve to introduce an element of hope and preference. Instead,

---

42 Samuel Ramos, *El perfil del hombre y la cultura de México*, 5th ed. (México: Espasa-Calpe Mexicana, 1972), p. 52.

43 Solomon Lipp, *Leopoldo Zea: From "Mexicanidad" to a Philosophy of History* (Waterloo, Ontario: Wilfrid Laurier University Press, 1980), Ch. 1, 2.

44 Octavio Paz, *El laberinto de la soledad*, 3rd ed. (México: Fondo de Cultura Económica, 1963), pp. 25–26.

the Spanish American is simply on guard, ready for anything that may emerge.[45] This "something" is part of his essence; it will inexorably transform him into what he is meant to be. It is this trait which is "authentically" Spanish American and constitutes his "originality". What this seems to reveal is a feeling that the Spanish American has not yet fully realized himself, a feeling born of inadequacy, of an historic inferiority complex.

The discovery of America, of the New World, led to the discovery of the Spanish American's awareness of himself, of his shortcomings, his place in universal history. There is no optimism here, nor pessimism either, for that matter. An optimistic note betokens hope for the future, a wish for something positive to happen. Expectancy, on the other hand, is neutral, without hope or fear. It is a posture, characterized by a lack of concern which admits of the possibility of being deceived or disillusioned. There is no sense in hoping for positive values, associated with the New World as the "kingdom of the future", since the future can also hold out a promise for Latin America as the victim of foreign imperialism. Does all this mean that the Spanish American is resigned to his fate, that he is a plaything in the hands of destiny? Not at all. To be prepared to expect is not the equivalent of being resigned. Mays Vallenilla thus attempts to combine the politics and economics of the New World with an existentialist posture which he attributes to its inhabitants.

* * *

The idea of America exerted its influence upon Spain, i.e., upon the idea which Spain had of itself. One need only refer to the Spanish American war to illustrate the point. The loss of Spain's last colonies in the New World, the "Disaster", as it was called, proved to be the catalyst which stimulated a group of intellectuals to delve into the nature of *Spanish* identity. Even the date of the "Disaster", 1898, was appropriated by this generation of writers. Its outstanding member, Miguel de Unamuno, joined the many commentators who attempted to analyze the Spanish personality, referring in passing, to undesirable traits, such as hatred and envy, to be found in various parts of Spain. Envy is not restricted to Spain alone, Unamuno goes on to say. It is also a basic ingredient of the Spanish American personality.[46]

Contemporary Spanish thinkers have reacted to the Spanish American phenomenon, specifically to the relationship between the mother country and her offspring. For example, José Luis Abellán, the noted historian of ideas, has reflected upon the idea of America. In comparing the colonization of Spanish America with that of the English venture, he suggests that the

45 Ernesto Mays Vellenilla, "El problema de América", in Leopoldo Zea, ed., *Antología de la filosofía americana contemporánea* (México: B. Costa Amic, 1968), pp. 215–25.

46 Miguel de Unamuno, "La envidia hispánica", in *Mi religión y otros ensayos*, 4th ed. (Madrid: Espasa-Calpe, 1964), p. 44.

former exhibited the characteristics of a military conquest. The English effort should be viewed solely in terms of a desire on the part of immigrants to settle and populate, and to practice their own form of religious worship. The Spaniards, on the other hand, were more interested in extending the political and religious power of the mother country.[47] Two other personalities deserve mention in this connection. Their opinions seem colored by their political orientation. Pedro Laín Entralgo remained in Spain after General Franco's victory in the Civil War, whereas José Gaos went into exile and, as a result, enriched the intellectual world of Mexico.

In his writings, Laín Entralgo sought to link the meaning of America to that of Spain, and to do so in more flexible, less doctrinaire manner than e.g., Ernesto Giménez Caballero, who was considered the chief theoretician of Spanish fascism, and who was, incidentally, rooted ideologically in Spain's imperial past. By contrast, in the decade which followed the end of the Civil War, Laín attempted to establish a dialogue with intellectuals opposed to the Franco regime. In a section of his work entitled "Europa, España, América",[48] Laín seeks to lay the intellectual groundwork of his thesis by affirming the three principal characteristics of European essence: classical antiquity, Christianity and elements of Germanic influence. These largely determined Europe's original mission, namely to universalize the Christian religion. Within this framework, Laín continues, Spain's task was crystal clear: to spearhead the European project, to implement, spread and defend Christianity – a program best described by the term "Hispanidad". How does Hispanic America fit into this formula? According to Laín, America has to embark upon this mission of "Hispanidad" and link its efforts with those of Spain.

Laín's idea of America is that it is an extension of Europe, performing the Christianizing mission with a view toward its universalization.[49] Moreover, he maintains, Spanish America will never be able to understand the history of its culture if it does not take into account the continual presence and influence of the mother country. Conversely, Spain can never solve its own cultural problems if Hispanic America is not included in a consideration of these problems and their possible solutions.

José Gaos illustrates the other extreme of the spectrum, namely, the group of Spanish intellectuals who could not remain in Spain after the defeat of the Spanish Republic. Nevertheless, Gaos did not consider himself an exile, but rather one who "moved" from one part of Spain to another. For him America was a part of Spain, possessing the same language and culture. In other words, Gaos merely "transferred" to Mexico (hence the term "trans-terrado" instead of "desterrado" as applied to himself), just as he had

---

47 José Luis Abellán, *La idea de América, idea y evolución* (Madrid: Istmo, 1972), p. 44.
48 Pedro Laín Entralgo, *España como problema* (Madrid: Aguilar, 1957), p. 675.
49 Laín Entralgo, p. 678.

previously gone to Madrid, for example, from his native Asturias; in short, a transfer from one cultural province to another. For Gaos the major concern was the more important problem of Spain's identity which had been called into question by the rest of Europe from which it felt alienated because of the Spanish Civil War.

Since America was considered a prolongation of Spain, it follows that the problem of American identity is viewed by Gaos as being linked with Spanish identity. Its corollary, the struggle for freedom, is a perennial one, and affects both Spain and Spanish America. Writing during the period of Franco's dictatorship, Gaos asserts that the Spanish American republics freed themselves from a mother country which had denied them the values which she herself had proclaimed at one time in the face of those who would deprive her of these self-same values. It was therefore incumbent upon Spain to emancipate herself. As Gaos puts it: "Spain is the last *Spanish American country* (my emphasis) which has to free itself from the common imperial past...as a people in the process of formation via fusion with others on the American continent after having resided on Iberian soil..."[50]

This argument is reminiscent of Leopoldo Zea's contention that the United States is opposed to liberating influences, as these apply to Spanish America, influences and values which the United States struggled at one time to achieve for itself, but not now, apparently, for others.

50 José Gaos, *En torno a la filosofía mexicana* (México, D.F.: Alianza Editorial Mexicana, 1980), p. 129.

7

THE UNITED STATES: PROBLEMS OF IDENTITY

The study of national character (see below, Appendix B), lends itself to a variety of approaches. Philosophers, novelists and literary critics are joined by historians, sociologists and psychologists. As far as the United States is concerned, all of these have had a field day. Furthermore, so-called biological or "racial" elements have been injected into the discussion to prove, for example, that Teutonic peoples have contributed to the strong sense of individual rights, freedom of thought and individual initiative associated with the Anglo-Saxon tradition. This has been countered by the "environmentalist" or historical perspective, as exemplified by Frederick Jackson Turner's "frontier thesis" (see below, Appendix A), which explains such character traits as restless, nervous energy and dominant individualism in terms of the influence of the North American frontier. In other words, the North American pioneer, possessed of a practical spirit, an exuberant feeling of liberty, and always quick to seize the initiative, is a product of the frontier. Unfortunately, this capacity has had its negative aspects as well. It can and has been used to justify expansion at the expense of other nations, as the "other" America can testify.

One may well ask in this connection: are the ideals of the American character centered in the past, as represented by Turner's agrarian frontier, or are they subject to modification, made necessary by the changing circumstances of contemporary industrial society? Are the distinctions of doctrines of the past in harmony with the pressures of the present? One may also ask: To what extent is the American character the result of the Puritan spirit of colonial days (see below Appendix C), combined with the pioneer spirit of the western frontier? One is tempted to speculate on the relative weight to be attached to each of these two strands which underlie the formation of the American personality prior to the nineteenth century. They form an interesting contrast: the Puritan ingredient with its rigid traditions and stern value system, and the pioneer of the nineteenth century who aggressively opened up the West, developing in the process all the character elements essential to an expanding economy.[1] Still

[1] Horace Kallen, *Culture and Democracy in the United States: Studies in the Group Psychology of the American People* (New York: Columbia University Press, 1924), p. 217.

another factor ought to be considered: the influx of European immigrants at the beginning of the twentieth century, which added to the tension between the agrarian and commercial lifestyles.

These immigrants provoked fears among the earlier arrivals, those of "native" stock, that the Anglo-Saxon character of the United States would suffer as a result of the presence of the more recent arrivals. Consequently, intensive "Americanization" programs were introduced. Immigrants were encouraged to attend evening classes in English and citizenship. This assimilation process, based on the "melting pot" theory, would, it was hoped, turn out "good" Americans. Although the program was implemented with considerable success, there were those who believed that immigrants could not be expected to forget their cultural heritage.[2] Continuing the use of the European mother tongue and elements of the foreign culture if so desired was not considered incompatible with developing into a patriotic American. This was essentially the position taken by the "cultural pluralists" who considered a knowledge of two or more languages an enriching experience. Indeed, it was thought that the emphasis on exclusively Anglo-Saxon values bordered on racism. This, then, was still another issue to be dealt with by U.S. liberals who were seeking to refine the principles of democracy.

Perhaps in this case a better term would have been "integration", rather than "assimilation". The latter term was associated with a complete erasing of "alien" cultural behavior, whereas "integration" implied a more flexible perspective, allowing for such behavior, if this was the desire of those concerned, while at the same time admitting a broader participation in the life of the adopted country. In the last analysis, the process, whatever it might be, would be affected by the passing of generations.

It was easy for the immigration issue to become a political football. "Nativist" opposition to newcomers, based on economic considerations, maintained that "American" character values were being destroyed by the influx of unassimilable foreigners. Character traits became confused with political values. Immigrants, it was charged, were incapable of using freedom and enjoying the benefits of democracy. They were weakening the original pioneering stock.

The reaction was not long in coming. Those who rose to the defense of immigrants maintained that the latter were idealistic; they respected education and culture. They had suffered persecution abroad and were therefore more appreciative than the "natives" of the values of American ideals. They did not take freedom for granted. Clearly, both sides of the argument suffered from excessive claims.

Within the context of this framework, the attempt to define the identity of the United States gave rise to three distinct groups of North Americans:

---

2   Louis Adamic, *From Many Lands* (New York: Harper, 1940).

1. The super-patriotic groups, such as the Daughters of the American Revolution and the American Legion, which insisted that their country was unique and separate vis-à-vis the other members of the world community. These groups tended to be isolationist in their political outlook; they believed that the United States was the only worthwhile model for the people of the world to follow.

2. Diametrically opposed was the group which adhered to what may be referred to as a universalist perspective. This group wished that the United States could become one with the rest of mankind.

3. Finally, there was the group which attempted to combine the most desirable elements of the other two groups, namely to develop both potential qualities in the North American character, i.e., whatever was unique as well as "universal".[3]

* * *

The dilemma experienced by significant segments of the United States is the painful realization of the gap that exists between the theoretical postulates of the American creed and the realities of North American life. There is a constant tug-of-war going on between the ideals of Lincoln and Walt Whitman, on the one hand, and the daily practices engaged in by a powerful financial empire, on the other. The forces which would like to see deep-rooted democratic traditions made real and applied to a maximum degree are continually frustrated by the ever-present spirit of acquisitiveness and aggressive competitiveness which often threatens to subvert democratic values. And yet it is this spirit of enterprise which has resulted in the creation of an astounding technology, and impressive economic and industrial progress.

It is perhaps this full-blown capitalist society of the United States that hardly rests on any foundation of an older culture which has given rise to the "cultured" anti-Americanism, still found in Europe and Latin America, a convenient weapon which supplements and reinforces the opposition to U.S. business practices. This would explain the "shallowness" of culture – a charge which is levelled at the United States in various parts of the world.

It should be borne in mind that this symptom, real or fancied, is linked historically to the absence of an aristocratic class in the United States. Democracy in that country, the result of a revolution against foreign injustice, rejected inherited privilege. Cultural activities, traditionally associated with the European aristocracy, were subsequently taken over by the bourgeoisie. It is therefore to the credit of the upper classes of the United States

3   Daniel J. Boorstin, *America and the Image of Europe* (New York: The World Publication Co. 1960), pp. 124–35.

that, despite the absence of an aristocratic cultural tradition, they made available countless funds for the promotion of intellectual activity. The pattern of large donations for this purpose can hardly be matched by other nations.

What do the inhabitants of the United States think of themselves? North Americans have always considered themselves unique and different from the rest of the world. Yet events were to contribute to the shattering of this uniqueness, especially since the beginning of the twentieth century.

For several decades the foreign policy of the United States was characterized by attempts to convince the world of its virtue and power. The "American way of life" was a slogan calculated to symbolize its competence and norms to be followed by the rest of the world. Unfortunately, at times, it tended to overestimate its capacity.

Especially at the close of the present century was the United States seen as a nation whose initial ideals were compromised for geo-political gain. As the dollar continued to control the value system, foreign enthusiasm for that nation waxed and waned at periodic intervals. Attitudes towards the United States continued to be ambivalent. American openness and friendliness were balanced by shallowness and crudity. (See Chapter 8 below.) The basic question to be addressed was whether U.S. citizens had themselves lost faith in some of the ideals associated with their country.

Many Americans are convinced of their military and economic superiority. The United States has established military bases in strategic areas of the world; it has opened McDonald and Kentucky Fried Chicken restaurants in various foreign countries, and flooded the world with its pop culture – all of these, symbols of might and marketing. Its gigantic industrial complex has always represented the promise of economic advance. However, in light of recent developments, the North American is no longer so sure of himself. Japan and Germany have been threatening U.S. superiority in this area. The irony of the situation should not be lost upon us. These two nations, rebuilt after World War II with U.S. economic aid, now believe that their standard of living is higher than that of their former enemy and that their culture and ethical values are superior.

As the North American character evolved in the course of the nineteenth century, certain characteristic traits began to be distinguished. The average citizen of the new republic was optimistic, possessed a sense of power. He emphasized material values, practicality and hard work. Culture, for him, had to be useful. Self-reliance and individualism assumed the dimensions of a national creed. However, as the nation entered the twentieth century, standardization seemed to displace individualism in importance. The North American still paid lip-service to democracy, equality and liberty, but loyalty became increasingly identified with conformity, especially during occasional periods of national hysteria. Democracy as an ideal was more political than socio-economic. Yet this seemed negated at times by those who identified democracy with egalitarianism – probably a residue of the Jacksonian era and a contributing factor to the opposition to any sign of a rigid caste system.

Native rebels and critics, in the early decades of the twentieth century, found much to criticize. They assailed the consequences produced by various historical strands which had evolved in the nation. Not only did they fire sardonic broadsides against the Puritanism of the 1920s which stressed conformity, moral compulsiveness and submission to the tyranny of public opinion. They also criticized mercilessly the provincialism and hypocrisy of the small town, associated with agrarian society.[4] In short, the United States did not need foreign culture critics. It had its own "debunkers", ever since Sinclair Lewis's ironic portrayal of Babbitt and H. L. Mencken's devastating criticism of the "booboisie", the "boobocracy" and standardized mediocrity. The machine, characteristic of the industrial age, added another ingredient to the personality configuration of the North American. According to Waldo Frank, it was responsible for fixing materialism firmly in the ethos of the nation, and creating an undesirable uniformity in its citizens.[5] Human sensibilities had become deadened under the weight of a crass materialism, the product of industrialism.

What seemed to be an outstanding defect on the American cultural scene, according to some of its notable critics, was the worship of success as the supreme value, the alpha and omega of human existence. Success was measured in terms of power, wealth, status and comfort. The drive to achieve success often transcended ethical considerations. Comfort was judged by how much one possessed. This, of course, was considerably removed from a state of comfort, which is simply the healthy equilibrium established between one's inner state of health and the outside world. Comfort, in the materialistic sense, requires one not only to maintain one's status, but to keep others from jeopardizing it. The resultant nervous tensions have made periodic visits to the psychiatrist a national pastime. Thus, one begins to wonder just how much comfort has been realized.

The American utilizes the machine in all its forms – the world of gadgetry in general – to increase the degree of his comfort. He finds that he has to keep up with the mad pace of his competitive existence. Consequently, he has to invent and improve new methods of comfort, to work more in order to earn more, so that he can buy more machines. He is thus engaged in a constant bartering process: exchanging comforts of doubtful value. He tends to become a slave of his own inventions. The machine has mastered him.

* * *

4   Thomas L. Hartshorne, *The Distorted Image* (Cleveland: The Press of the Case Western Reserve University, 1968), p. 90.

5   Waldo Frank, *El redescubrimiento de América*, 2nd ed. (Madrid: Revista de Occidente, 1930). Translated from the English by J. Héctor de Zeballa.

In recent decades, it has become evident that there is an increasing tendency to move away from attempts to define national character, and to analyze instead the principles of the value system of the United States. The presence of totalitarian regimes in various parts of the world have proved to be an additional stimulus in this direction. Americans are convinced that the United States, with all its faults, is still a better place to live in than a military dictatorship.

The many negative attitudes manifested toward the United States are believed by the Americans themselves to be due to envy. It is basically envy that lies at the base of all the antagonism and resentment engendered. Generally speaking, the average citizen of the United States does not look upon his country as an imperialist nation, but rather as the leader in the defense of the "free world", a vestige of "cold war" rhetoric. He believes that it is the continual jockeying for advantageous positions which has dictated U.S. policy abroad, of which the Spanish American case is just one of many examples.

Intimately connected with the North American's pride in his country is the feeling which he cherishes toward his institutions. A mid-nineteenth-century commentator observes that the American's feelings are more centered upon his institutions than his country. "His affections have more to do with the social and political system with which he is connected than with the soil which he inhabits."[6] Every American, according to this observer, feels intimately involved in the success of democracy as a political system. Indeed, American patriotism is dependent upon democracy.

Regrettably, the early ideal of the United States, the land of hope and promise, seems to have lost its mythical dimensions, and has become, especially for many Spanish Americans, a source of disillusionment, and eventually, of fear and hostility. It seems that many North Americans, in spite of their lip-service and even firm belief in the American creed and its glorification of equality, opportunity and democratic lifestyle, believe in these values only in a restricted sense. When Americans of the South aspire to attain these values for themselves, those of the North have placed obstacles of all sorts in their path. United States interests have proved more powerful than abstract ideals.

* * *

In considering the problem of national identity in the United States, one must also take into account the socio-political setting. The United States is not being utilized by foreign powers; its population does not face the same problems as, for example, those which confront the inhabitants of Spanish

---

6 Alexander Mackay in *America in Perspective*, ed. Henry Steele Commager (New York: Random House, 1947), p. 112.

America. Identity is not defined chiefly in terms of struggle, although this element may also be present, in less obvious measure. Ethnicity would seem to play a larger role insofar as the question of "Who is an American?" is concerned.

In a multicultural society like the United States, the development of a pluralistic personality may be expected. Individuals are at liberty to make as much or as little of their ethnic origins as they please. Even if an individual chooses to disregard his ethnic origins, he may still reveal certain ethnic elements in his behavior. This will not, in any way, diminish his identity as an American.

Historically, as has been pointed out, American identity in the United States has always been linked to the problem of immigrants and their assimilation into the dominant culture. In the early decades of the twentieth century "Americanization" implied assimilation of all immigrant groups into a uniform national type. It was hoped that "hyphenated" Americans would eventually disappear, and that the United States would become ever more homogeneous. What was overlooked, perhaps, was that it was difficult to drop ethnic attributes and loyalties within a relatively short period of time.

There was an additional drawback. The "old" Anglo-Saxon Americans expected the immigrants to give up their ethnic differences, but were reluctant to accept them even after this had been accomplished. Theoretically, such an attitude violated the basic tenets of the American creed which was grounded in the English tradition of freedom. To be American, one merely had to commit oneself to a political set of beliefs which stressed freedom, equality and republicanism. Cultural differences could not be allowed to become a source of conflict. The ideal was one of a unified, even though ethnically diverse, society.[7]

Nevertheless, the so-called hyphenated American continued to present difficulties. In some cases the phenomenon of the Irish-American and the German-American, for example, tended to grow weaker with each succeeding generation, as the effects of assimilation made themselves felt. However, in some cases, probably because of a greater degree of visibility of ethnic differences, prejudice continued unabated. This was especially the case with the more recent arrivals to the United States, e.g., Vietnamese, Korean, Chinese, Indians, etc., making the process of "Americanization" more difficult.

Despite the efforts of well-intentioned groups to counteract ethnic prejudice, the virus still persists, at best in subtle forms in various social situations. In the worst of circumstances, it flares up at intervals, depending on the frequency and intensity of pressure points that result in overt friction between dominant culture groups and ethnic minorities, or among the ethnic

7 Nathan Glazer, *Ethnic Dilemmas* (Cambridge, Mass.: Harvard University Press, 1983), p. 336.

minorities themselves; for example, Italo-Americans against Blacks, Blacks
against Orientals and Hispanics. Anti-Black prejudice and Anti-Semitism
are, of course, not restricted to any one group. Ironically, too, American
Indians are often the targets of "native" Americans. All of these negative
elements, exacerbated in times of social and economic crisis, are roadblocks
in the process of developing a feeling which is conducive to healthy, national
well-being.

Yet the positive elements should not be ignored. For example, where
Americanism took on economic trappings, it was defined, to a great extent,
in terms of the visible contrasts between the immigrant dweller of the impoverished city and his children, who had, through upward social mobility,
achieved economic success and were now residing in high-rise condomi-
niums or in suburban homes which they had purchased.

"If you don't like it, why don't you go back where you came from?"
became the favorite dart, aimed at those who did not conform exactly to the
prevailing mores of the "older" Americans. Thus, social and political intolerance, racial and religious discrimination, vandalism and terrorism, could
get along quite comfortably with "Americanism".

The increase in population shifts, especially from East to West, has tended
to complicate the acculturation process for countless numbers of arrivals to
the New World. For example, the United States and Canada have in recent
times experienced new waves of immigrants from Latin America, the
Middle East, Asia and Eastern Europe. The difficulties experienced by
ethnic minorities have multiplied, all of which has brought into sharper
focus the problem of ethnicity within a dominant culture.

Ethnicity, by definition, implies a sense of peoplehood which is experienced by many sub-groups in the United States. It can be diminished or
emphasized depending on circumstances. American identity in the sense in
which the term is used in the United States is ideally more inclusive than
ethnic identity – although some would argue the point – because it is more
universal and partakes of a more abstract quality. It should be remembered in
this connection that the European Enlightenment transformed the original
English liberties into universal principles. U.S. identity should, therefore, not
be equated with Wasp ethnicity, nor does it belong to any one cultural
grouping. Immigrants do not have to be "Waspified". In fact, the Anglo-
Saxon element can also be considered as an ethnic group which happened to
take an earlier boat to get to the States.

* * *

The policy of "Americanization" tended to develop political overtones. It
evolved into a reactionary chauvinism, linked to Anglo-Saxon racism, and
embarked upon a campaign against foreign radicalism. For example, after
World War I immigrant workers were associated with bolshevism and

anarchism, and were often hounded by the police. As a reaction to this development, cultural pluralism became that much more attractive. As noted, it encouraged immigrants to retain elements of their heritage. However, eventually these immigrants and their descendants would become acculturated. The basic assumption of the cultural pluralist was that a new and superior culture would result, one which would combine the best of all cultures. A second premise assumed that a state of harmony would always exist among the different ethnic groups, an assumption the validity of which has still to be realized.[8]

Thus the ethnic factor moved to the foreground and began to play a significant role in the determination of national identity. Democratic principles were utilized by ethnic minorities to further their claims. As the twentieth century wore on, Chicanos, native Indians, Blacks and Puerto Ricans emerged to make demands upon the national conscience.

An interesting question arises in this connection: If some of these demands are granted, will such action tend to make these ethnic minorities more group-conscious and consequently impede acculturation or integration into U.S. society? What does this say for national identity? A related question could be: Would not such a policy affect other ethnic groups? Would they also begin to make special demands?[9] How long a step is it, in this respect, from national identity to national unity? Will diversity threaten unity?

At present the world is witness to a recrudescence of autonomous and separatist tendencies. For example, in Canada the provinces are seeking greater powers, thus weakening the effectiveness of the Federal government in Ottawa. In the former Soviet Union individual republics have broken away from Moscow's control. Yugoslavia has been torn apart. Will centrifugal forces prove stronger in the United States as well?

In accordance with the principle of dynamism referred to repeatedly in this essay, the U.S. personality, its "type" or "essence" and value system, will continue to undergo modification as the years go by and we enter the twenty-first century. For example, the ethnic nature of the population is expected to change considerably in the coming decades.

The prognosis advanced by authorities in the field of demographic change is that by the middle of the twenty-first century, Hispanic and non-white racial groups will outnumber descendants of the "original" western European Caucasian stock. The so-called "typical" White American will become a minority group. Statistics indicate that the birth rate among African Americans, Hispanics and Asians is considerably higher than that of White

8 William Peterson, Michael Novak, and Philip Gleason, *Concepts of Ethnicity* (Cambridge, Mass.: Harvard University Press, 1982), p. 142.
9 Glazer, p. 284.

Americans who trace their descent to Europe.[10] One may ask at this point: Just how much cultural conflict would result if this development goes forward? Would the goals and aspirations of the African Americans, for example, be identical to those of the "Hispanics", the Vietnamese, or the "whites"? How would all this affect the concept of cultural or national identity of the North Americans?

A built-in difficulty in the very heart of the American value system, one which requires continual harmonious adjustment, involves two basic principles: liberty and equality. These seem to make for conflict, since liberty produces differences in both individuals and groups, and equality attempts to diminish them. The American creed will, in the years to come, be subjected to severe tests in the face of radical demographic changes. It will have to be nurtured and strengthened. It is to be hoped that its ideals and principles will be applied to a broader spectrum and become more universalized than is the case at present.

How this question reflects upon national values and cultural identity becomes a problem fraught with difficulties. How to maintain a distinct national identity in the face of a constantly increasing ethnic challenge, calls for courage, ingenuity, and tolerance in attempting to reduce the number of friction points, and effect a harmonious equilibrium that will satisfy the emotional needs of each group within a larger cultural framework which strives to preserve the American "essence".

Truly, "E Pluribus Unum", which appears on United States coins, will assume a richer meaning in the light of this development. Ironically enough, the Mexican philosopher, José Vasconcelos, who was quite antagonistic toward the United States, and who coined the phrase "cosmic race", to be formed ideally in a future Latin America, would have been aghast in the face of this unexpected transformation: all the elements of the "cosmic race" would seem to have a much better prospect of coalescing in the United States than Vasconcelos had ever imagined.

The United States continues to be redefined. Immigration has furnished the country with new talent and energy – a policy in line with the inspiring words of Emma Lazarus, inscribed at the base of the Statue of Liberty. The United States can profit from the contributions made by people coming from many lands. This is the positive side of the coin. Yet the negative aspect should not be overlooked. Periods of change can be unsettling and can produce painful conflicts with resultant unpleasant consequences.

Admittedly, it is more difficult to govern a multicultural society than one which is relatively homogeneous. Non-white groups, with a strong attachment to their respective cultural values, will project their attitudes in various

[10] If current trends in immigration and birth rates continue, it is estimated that by the end of the twentieth century the Hispanic population will have increased by 21%, Blacks by 12%, and Whites by 2%; William A. Henry III, "Beyond the Melting Pot", *Time*, April 9, 1990, p. 38.

areas of the dominant cultural scene. For example, Hispanic elements of the population have been demanding that Spanish be made one of the two official languages in Florida and California. In the latter state a backlash has resulted which declares English to be the only official language recognized by the state. What does this mean for cultural identity in the United States? In the field of education, ethnic minorities are questioning the content of textbooks used in the teaching of history. Many books accepted as classics are viewed as being instruments of "cultural imperialism". University courses in Black studies often adopt a revisionist approach, claiming – and rightly so – that greater emphasis should be placed on the contribution of Blacks to the development of the United States. In this context, for example, Martin Luther King means more than the Pilgrims and Plymouth Rock.

The potential points of friction between cultural identity and national awareness are best illustrated by the situation described above. Perhaps this is to be expected in a nation which is home to various cultural minorities. In this case the challenge is one of attempting to adjust the cultural traditions of the ethnic minority to the value system of the dominant national group. The principle of harmonious integration recognizes that not only should the nation respect the identity if its minorities, but also that the latter participate in, and identify with, the cultural life of the national territory wherein they reside.

The principle of harmonious integration must avoid two extremes: 1. on the one hand, enforced assimilation which would insist that ethnic minorities forget their cultural heritage in the process of identifying with dominant culture patterns; 2. ethnic isolation, in order to maintain the language and traditions of the minority culture. A cultural minority should not be reluctant to expose itself to the influences of encircling contacts because of a fear of losing something of itself in the process. The Cuban who refuses to speak English in the United States, the Quebec separatist who bans English signs, the Anglophone who is opposed to the use of French in his Canadian province are all – regardless of how sincere their motivation may be – guilty of cultural barbarism. The ideal, in short, is one of establishing and maintaining a delicate balance, a harmonious synthesis, which makes possible a pluralistic cultural identity. An individual who speaks two languages, said Goethe, is equal to two persons.

Finally, let us note some ambiguities in rounding out the discussion on United States identity.

In the first place, many groups that have suffered discrimination in the past in the areas of education, housing and occupation, have since progressed to a degree that would be unthinkable if the United States were the racist society which many think it is.[11]

---

11 Glazer, p. 12. Note, however, that manifestations of racism in the United States have, of late, acquired an increased measure of frequency and intensity. Instances of police brutality,

Many white elements in the United States seem to exhibit ambivalent attitudes. Their moral conscience places them on the side of African Americans and the Hispanics. However, when the latter make progress which seems "excessive, there is a tendency to over-react negatively. This is because the "progress" made has come too close for comfort. Only time and re-education of attitudes will contribute to improving this situation.

One must be sufficiently mature to distinguish between diversity and divisiveness. Acceptance of all groups on an equal basis and tolerance of ethnic diversity constitute the essence of Americanism. A similar distinction should be made between uniformity and unity. The former implies sameness, the latter allows for diversity.

Of course, what is presented here is the ideal. Americans do not fully live up to it. The traditional position maintains that the U.S. value system is good. United States citizens are committed to it. However, there are too many examples which serve to negate this assertion (Viet Nam, Watergate, Nicaragua, etc.); these provide ammunition to ideological opponents who maintain that the American creed is a sham, a smokescreen, used to cover up a system of exploitation.[12]

It is obvious that the multicultural approach should be incorporated at all levels of the educational curriculum. It should add to and supplement that which exists, not replace it. A flexible perspective will stress not only the origin and beginnings of the American value system; it must also address the forward direction in which the nation is travelling and the goals to be achieved.

Yet one central point must be remembered. When immigrants arrive, they should be (and many are) committed to United States values. This is why they came in the first place. They can maintain their loyalty to the cultural values of the old country in addition to those of the new land, and above all, be aware of what it means to be an American. If not, the result may well be a "Balkanization" of the United States, something to be avoided and resisted, regardless of whether the hitherto dominant group of whites becomes a minority in the future.

Sensitive Americans are aware of the ulcers which are still to be found in their society. Open wounds continue to fester; tragic conditions cry out for improvement. A good deal has already been accomplished. Much more remains to be done. Concern in this area on the national scene may be interpreted as a healthy sign. The shock waves experienced nation-wide – e.g., in the area of race relations – may be birth pangs, a prelude to the

---

coupled with worsening conditions of poverty among the Black population, have resulted in bloody riots. These have occurred in various cities of the United States, especially in areas populated by African Americans e.g., Los Angeles, California.

12 Peterson, et al., p. 135.

process which the nation is undergoing on the road to becoming an authentic multicultural and multiracial society.

If there is any complaint that the American creed is one thing and American practice quite another, and that the two are not in phase with each other, then the rejoinder must be that the United States, like any other organism, is still evolving. Admittedly, actual fact is very different from the dream. However, it must be remembered that ideals, principles and creeds, by definition, are never realized to perfection. They are guide lines and can only be striven for and approximated to an optimum degree. That, after all, is the very nature of an ideal.

8

SPANISH AMERICANS VIEW
THE UNITED STATES

A random sampling of the works of Spanish Americans essayists will reveal considerable variation in judgment and evaluation concerning the nature of the two Americas, as well as the personality configuration of their respective inhabitants. Spanish American thinkers, perhaps even more so than European commentators, had good reason to record their impressions of the "Colossus" which cast its shadow over the continent to the south. Commentaries were often one-sided (whether positive or negative). At times, as can be expected, a given writer would change his point of view considerably with the passage of time.

To begin with, a decidedly positive attitude vis-à-vis the United States was manifested by José Victorino Lastarria of Chile who was one of the outstanding representatives of the group that advocated a complete break with Spain, culturally speaking, after Independence had been won. He speaks of the critical political conditions in which the nation finds itself and refers to the philosophy of self-government, characteristic of the United States, which Chile would do well to emulate. He contrasts the absolute monarchy of Spain with the democratic republic of the north.

Lastarria was one of many Spanish American intellectuals, influenced by European Romanticism. However, for him the most important facet of the Romantic movement was the struggle for freedom and rejection of the Spanish heritage. The new America had to break with the past, and the past was Spain. Lastarria belongs to that group of thinkers that considered the United States to be the ideal model to be followed in the realm of political thought. So pro-U.S. was he that when his son was born, he named him Washington.[1]

Comparing the Old World with the new, Lastarria affirms that in Europe the principle of authority dominates all spheres of society. The individual and society exist for the State. By contrast, in America "democracy tends to

---

[1] William Rex Crawford, *A Century of Latin American Thought* (Cambridge: Harvard University Press, 1945), p. 59.

destroy the principle of authority which is based on force and privilege, but which strengthens that principle when it is supported by justice in the interests of society".[2]

Comparing the two Americas from this point of view, Lastarria asserts that "in the North the people are sovereign in law and in fact; the law is administered and the people's interests safeguarded by their representatives. In Spanish America, the people as such do not exist, except for the glory and profit of their absolute and natural lord, the King of Spain".[3]

Europe, then, for Lastarria, is authoritarian; America is democratic. True authority in America rests on justice and operates in the interests of society. Europe would do well, he continues, to imitate America, if it wishes to save itself. The light of democracy now travels from west to east; unfortunately, Europe shuts its eyes and refuses to see it.[4] We are, above all, Americans, which is to say, democrats, and therefore we must be prepared to forge our future without imitating European models in blind and uncritical fashion. Just as Europe has to look to America for its salvation, Spanish America must look to the north in order to improve the human condition.

Lastarria laments the fact that Europe does not know America; in fact, Europe looks down upon the new continent. Democracy is the shining light that emanates from America and Europe ignores it at its own risk. Lastarria is highly annoyed, since America does not ignore Europe, but, rather, studies her continually.

With respect to his own country Lastarria believes that North America should replace Europe as a model to be emulated. "We have to rebuild the social sciences," he writes, "as the Anglo Americans have done; to accept blindly the European traditions...to transplant them exactly, without deliberation, is to go counter to our regeneration, to retard it, causing it to deviate from its natural course."[5]

Interestingly enough, Lastarria was opposed to the formation of a union of Spanish American nations in order to resist the power and influence of North America. It was therefore logical that he should justify and support the Monroe Doctrine, especially in light of the French adventure in Mexico, involving the Maximilian episode. The Monroe Doctrine, in the words of Lastarria, could be considered a "precedent of International Law for the defense of America".[6]

Like his contemporaries, Sarmiento and Alberdi, Lastarria favored Euro-

2 José Victorino Lastarria, "Europa Autoritaria y América Democrática", *Lastarria*, ed. Luis Enrique Délano (México: Ediciones de la Secretaría de Educación Pública, 1944), p. 63.

3 Norman P. Sacks, "José Victorino Lastarria y Henry Thomas Buckle: El positivismo, La Historia de España", in *Estudios sobre José Victorino Lastarria* (Santiago: Ediciones de la Universidad de Chile, 1988), pp. 147–48.

4 Lastarria, "Europa Autoritaria...", p. 65.

5 Lastarria, "Europa Autoritaria...", p. 67.

6 Sacks, p. 149.

pean immigration as being beneficial to the development of the Latin American continent. Naturally, he insisted that the immigrant come with financial resources, initiative and healthy work habits. Again, pointing to the United States as an example, he insists that the immigrant integrate into society, as is the case in the North, and not form separate colonies, antagonistic to the interests of Spanish America.

Lastarria's pupil, Francisco Bilbao, was even more radical in his condemnation of Spain and glorification of the United States, although his pro-U.S. attitude changed considerably after the U.S.–Mexican War. In an extremely Romantic vein, Bilbao reacted harshly against the Spanish Catholic tradition of intolerance. His lyricism is unrestrained, especially when he extols the freedom of thought, characteristic of the United States. This freedom, he writes, is inseparable from the origin and development of the nation to the North. All of its prosperity, political life, indeed its very sovereignty, are inextricably bound up with and dependent upon freedom of thought.[7] He hopes that the influence of the United States will result in a synthesis of American civilization, destined to rejuvenate the Old World.[8]

In his *América en peligro*, this Chilean firebrand proclaims that Catholicism is the religion of Latin America. This is incompatible with the idea of a republic, which is the case in the United States. Catholicism, according to Bilbao's reasoning, denies the basic principle of the Republic, namely, the sovereignty of reason, found in every individual. Republican doctrine, on the other hand, is opposed to dogma which imposes blind obedience. This, then, is essentially the tragic dilemma which confronts Spanish America: either Catholicism triumphs and, with it, the Monarchy and theocracy; or Republicanism wins, directed freely by human reason.[9]

The choice is obvious: Either Spanish America embarks upon the road to Rome, or it follows the example of the United States where free inquiry is the lifeblood of the nation. What divides the New World is the conflict posed by the religion of obedience, pain and grace, versus that of freedom, joy and justice.

At times, Bilbao is carried away by his own eulogies, as for example, when he refers to the Puritans in a somewhat naive manner: "These Puritans, or their children, have presented to the world the most beautiful of Constitutions, which guides the destinies of the greatest, richest, wisest and freest of peoples. That nation is today in history what Greece was – the shining light of the world, the last word in time, the most positive revelation of the divine in philosophy, art and politics. That nation has given us this word: *self-government*, as the Greeks have given us *autonomy*. And what is

[7]   Francisco Bilbao, *El evangelio americano* (Santiago: Ercilla, 1941), pp. 60–62.
[8]   Benjamín Subercasseaux, "Visión de Estados Unidos y América en la Elite Liberal (1860–70)", *Cuadernos Americanos*, 130, No. 3 (May–June, 1980), p. 128.
[9]   Francisco Bilbao, *La América en Peligro* (Santiago: Ercilla, 1940).

even better: they practise what they say, they put into practice what they think, and they create what is necessary for the moral and material perfection of the human species."[10]

Pro- and anti-U.S. sentiment in Spanish America continued to see-saw in accordance with the historical circumstances of the moment. The U.S.-Mexican war alarmed Spanish Americans who feared the threat of the powerful nation to the north. On the other hand, the Civil War in the United States and the struggle against slavery produced sympathetic attitudes.

In the interest of historical truth it should be pointed out that the expansionist policies of the United States did not meet with unanimous approval in that country. For example, the Mexican war was opposed by some highly-placed personalities in the government. President Lincoln declared that it was a war which was unnecessary and unconstitutional. General Ulysses S. Grant condemned it as "one of the most unjust military operations which the strong have ever undertaken against the weak".[11]

The inevitable march of history soon tipped the scales. Pro-U.S. sentiment in Spanish America gave way to acerbic criticism of United States foreign policy, especially after the Spanish American War. The United States had been hailed as a beacon of democratic thought; its Revolution had inspired, at least in part, the movement for Independence throughout Spanish America. Now the situation, according to Spanish Americans, had changed. They reflected bitterly that the so-called American credo, so deeply ingrained in the psyche of the United States, the emphasis on the democratic philosophy of life, freedom of association, individual initiative, and the right to engage in private enterprise, were somehow not considered applicable to their own countries. United States economic interests dictated otherwise. If the new Spanish American nations were allowed to compete in the world markets, if indeed they were capable of doing so, they would threaten the economic activities of the north. From the point of view of the latter, it was preferable that the Spanish Americans constitute the "backyard" of the United States. In the eyes of the aggressive, industrial enterprises, Spanish America was simply a market to be exploited, a fact which was destined to hinder the development of the continent. Furthermore, the Balkanization of Spanish America, the existence of a score of mutually suspicious countries, was advantageous only to those who could profit by continuing to foment whatever differences might exist among them.

* * *

10 Bilbao, *El evangelio americano*, p. 61.
11 José Agustín Balseiro, *Expresión de Hispanoamérica*, 2nd rev. ed. (Madrid: Gredos, 1970), p. 46.

Scores of Spanish American thinkers appeared on the literary landscape. Critical commentaries concerning the United States were featured in the press, some of which compared that country with Spanish America, culturally and politically. For example, José Martí viewed the two Americas as being complementary. Each represents only a partial view of life, he wrote. Perhaps they will, one day, learn from each other. It is imperative for the United States to know us, he argued. The hostile attitude evinced toward us by our powerful neighbor is the greatest danger facing Spanish America. Disdain can be dissipated only by mutual understanding. Nevertheless, the materialism of the United States continues to be excessive. Any nation which lacks a spiritual foundation is bound to deteriorate.

As a correspondent for Spanish American periodicals, Martí recorded his impressions of people and events, while living in New York. These were, on the whole, favorable and sympathetic. Unfortunately, only one sentence seems to have been remembered in Spanish America: "I know the monster since I have lived in its entrails." Even though he believed that "Latins and Saxons are equally capable of harboring virtues and defects",[12] he nevertheless maintained that the United States had lost ground since Independence. The North American of his day was less human and virile, while the Spanish American was superior, compared to what he had been when he emerged from the colonial period.[13]

Although Martí has been claimed by both pro- and anti-U.S. elements in Spanish America, the latter seem to be winning the contest. Martí admired Abraham Lincoln, but warned against United States expansionism. The United States, he thought, believed that liberty was its exclusive possession. Martí, like Bolívar, dreamed of freedom for the entire continent. His dream encompassed one grand confederation of Spanish American republics, characterized by three sets of forces which would operate continually. These forces might best be represented by three concentric circles. As one proceeded from the center, moving in an outward direction, one would pass from the national, through the continental, and finally, arrive at the universal. The larger circle would always encompass and affect the smaller.

The nature of the governments of Spanish America also concerned him. He was opposed to imitation of forms of government, based on foreign models. The governments of Spanish America, he wrote, must be based on the realities which exist in each country, i.e., the cultural heritage, the native traditions and institutions. "The individual who would govern well in America is not the one who knows how the German or French government is run, but rather, one who is aware of the nature of the diverse elements of

---

[12] José Martí, "La verdad sobre los Estados Unidos", in *Páginas escogidas* (Havana: Instituto Cubano del Libro, 1971), p. 387.

[13] Martí, p. 392.

which his country is constituted..."[14] In short, a Spanish American government should be a natural outgrowth of the country, and not merely a shadow of other nations, an echo of other voices.[15] The imitation of foreign models can even extend to matters of dress. "We were a mask," Martí exclaims indignantly, "wearing breeches from England, Parisian vests, North American jackets, and Spanish caps."[16]

Perhaps the best known pro-U.S. Spanish American personality is Domingo Faustino Sarmiento, the "Educator-President" of Argentina. Friend of the New England educator, Horace Mann, and admirer of the educational system of the United States, he attempted to "civilize" his country by introducing educational reforms. He proposed to emulate the United States in an effort to rid Argentina and the continent, in general, of the "barbaric" and backward conditions that prevailed in his day. The United States, according to Sarmiento, was advancing with gigantic strides along the road to political freedom and economic prosperity.

When Sarmiento arrived in the United States in 1847, he was tremendously impressed by the strength and energy he encountered. He had dreamed of an ideal society, and he believed he had finally found it in this country, a land that was rich, free, enterprising and enlightened. What he admired especially was the democratic system of government which he was to contrast continually with the tyranny and ignorance of Spanish America.

In June 1868 the University of Michigan bestowed upon him the honorary degree of Doctor of Laws. On this occasion he referred in glowing terms to "that great school, the United States of America". Furthermore, he went on to say, "we are a young nation which has had to make and re-make everything during its short national existence. We are the children of a nation (Spain) which was unable to give us or teach us what she did not have or even know about. In that respect we were less fortunate than you, the children of the Puritans, who have inherited a lesson and have splendidly taken advantage of it, without having to undergo long years of struggle in order to exchange your rude colonial raiment for the proud tunic of democracy..."[17]

Sarmiento does not miss the opportunity to remind his audience (slyly perhaps?) at these Commencement exercises that, unlike the United States, his country, on winning its independence, "did not leave for the future overwhelming problems, such as slavery, the solution of which cost

14 José Martí, "Nuestra América", in Carlos Ripoll, *Conciencia Intelectual de América* (New York: Las Américas, 1966), p. 226.
15 Leopold Zea, *Precursores del pensamiento latinoamericano contemporáneo* (México: Sep Diana, 1979), pp. 20–21.
16 Martí, in Ripoll, p. 229.
17 From an eye-witness report, written by Bartolomé Mitre y Vedia (1845–1900), son of ex-President Mitre, and Sarmiento's secretary, in a letter dated Sept. 10, 1886. The letter was written originally in Genoa, Italy, and published subsequently in *La Nación* of Buenos Aires.

hundreds of thousands of lives and thousands of millions of dollars".[18] Finally, in a somewhat boastful vein, he affirms that as soon as Argentina rids itself of tyrannical rule, its law will assure forever the freedom of all of its inhabitants. The next day Sarmiento left for Buenos Aires to become President of Argentina.

As is well known, Sarmiento's main thesis, advanced in his *Facundo*, explains Argentina's condition in terms of geographic determinism. The country, as opposed to the city, represents disorder and barbarism. The inhabitants of the Pampas do not know the meaning of law and civilization. The vastness of the Pampa produces a feeling of insecurity and stoic resignation in the face of death. In contrast, only the cities are aware of the guiding principles of social solidarity, and of the rights and duties of the nation's citizens. The nature of Argentine history is explained by the physical and social environment and the way these mould the personality of the rural inhabitant. On the other hand, the educated classes in the city represent civilization. For example, the *Salón Literario* of Buenos Aires which encouraged the reading of predominantly French books, was considered to exemplify civilization, European culture, to be more precise, in contrast to Americanism and anti-Europeanism which were equated with barbarism. In short, in Sarmiento's thinking, Argentina's Europeanized future was locked in battle with the backward Americanism of past and present. This polarity eventually broadened into a conflict between commerce and progress, on the one hand, and economic and cultural stagnation on the other.

At times there appears to be an irresistible oscillation which takes hold of Sarmiento – an oscillation between the political and the esthetic. On the political side, he wants to attack the centers of barbarism that he believes exist in the vast plains of the interior and in the customs and institutions of rural society. But on the other, esthetic side he pays hommage to the natural environment and picturesque way of life of his native country. The men of the Pampa could have been poets and dreamers. From a practical point of view he condemns the gauchos as a retarded social element; yet his romantic impulses well up within him as he describes, with no small measure of admiration and in the most colorful of terms, the lifestyle of the various types of gauchos. Perhaps Sarmiento himself was soon to realize that his formula was not hard and fast. The truth was that the plains were not so barbarian, nor the cities so civilized as he had made them out to be.

Sarmiento looked upon the United States as the great Europeanizing agent. The trouble with Argentina, he wrote, is its size. The cities are small islands of civilization; the pampa surrounds them and laps at them like a sea of barbarism. The United States, on the other hand, is an outstanding example of a civilized country, successful in avoiding a rigid social class

---

18   Mitre y Vedia, op. cit.

system, and a nation which is making phenomenal progress in the direction of political freedom and economic well-being. North America was, for Sarmiento, the land of hope; it would realize its aspirations through education. When he returned to Argentina after having visited the United States, he praised that nation as one which had established true democracy and had made all classes and races equal. He had seen the perfect country, energetic and productive. Education was the panacea for his country's ills, and the United States was outstanding in educational matters. Without education there could be no free people or democratic institutions. Yet he believed that Spanish America should not imitate slavishly. What he wished was to shake off Spanish influence and to Europeanize. To achieve this, Sarmiento, the ideological spokesman of the rising bourgeoisie, attempted a transfer of the lifestyle of the middle class of the United States, as a model to be followed by his native Argentina.

Regrettably, in later years, he was less than kind to Spanish American society. Influenced by Positivist thought which emphasized science and technique as a method of building civilization, he attributed the lack of progress in this direction to the racial inferiority of Spanish America. He speaks of the superiority of the Caucasian race and maintains that it is necessary to diminish the role of the indigenous population; the white race is the most intelligent and progressive.[19]

The colonization of the Americas offers a striking contrast for Sarmiento. The English colonists excluded the Indians from their society, whereas the Spaniards absorbed them. Sarmiento thus establishes, at least to his own satisfaction, the superiority of North American society, attributed to resistance to miscegenation. Thus, for Sarmiento, the United States is the ideal society, a product of racial purity. He could never have imagined that a century later this nation would resemble an ethnic mosaic of the most varied colors.[20]

Swept along by the winds of Social Darwinism of his time, Sarmiento justifies the elimination of the indigenous population. "...The strong races exterminate the weak, the civilized peoples replace the savages in appropriating the land."[21] Sarmiento, the "great educator" seems to have violated his own principles. He has overlooked the fact that the Indian, too, is capable of being educated in the developmental process of humankind. For Sarmiento, the Indian represents barbarism; he must be eliminated before progress of any kind can be achieved.

* * *

19 Roberto Fernández Retamar, *Calibán cannibale* (Paris: François Maspero, 1973), p. 102.
20 Antonio Sacuto, "El indio en la obra literaria de Sarmiento y Martí", *Cuadernos Americanos*, No. 156 (Jan. Feb. 1968), p. 160.
21 Domingo F. Sarmiento, "Conflicto y armonías de las razas en América", in *Obras*, 5th ed. (Buenos Aires: Espasa-Calpe, 1939), p. 214.

Sarmiento's thesis, as an attempt to analyze the nature of Argentina and its inhabitants, was attacked vigorously by his compatriot, Juan Bautista Alberdi. Sarmiento, argued Alberdi, did not understand the role played by economic factors. In Alberdi's view, Sarmiento believed that the Argentine revolution was a movement inspired by ideas, rather than material interests; that the countryside, i.e., the provinces of the interior, was devoid of ideas, and that only the cities, chiefly Buenos Aires, played host to educational endeavors.

Alberdi defends the hinterland. It is there that raw materials are produced and wealth created. The provinces thus provided the necessary power to promote the Revolution. Alberdi does not mince words: "If only Sarmiento had suspected that the nature of political power resides in the power of finance, then he would not have wasted his time, prattling his stupid and ridiculous theories of civilization and barbarism, of city and country."[22]

Alberdi advocated the importation of machinery and the fostering of immigration, but his dream was not to be realized. Foreign capital did not modernize Latin America. It was invested in accordance with the necessities of the foreign investors, specifically, the world market. These were interested in the *utilization* of the Latin American continent, not its development. As a result, the Latin American bourgeoisie exercised the role of consumer, rather than producer. It became an intermediary, and dependent upon the international bourgeoisie.

Alberdi also emphasized the historic role played by England and the United States in his program for social and economic development of South America. Although his observations are directed primarily at satisfying the needs of his own country, they could also be applied to the continent as a whole. "To govern is to populate" is the much quoted slogan, taken from his voluminous work, the *Bases*, which is an outline for the future development of Argentina. Yet the phrase requires an explanation. Alberdi employs the term in the sense – he says – that to populate is to educate, to improve, to civilize, to enrich and make great, spontaneously and rapidly, as has happened in the United States. Furthermore, Alberdi would like the great mass of immigrants to come from England; English is the language of liberty, industry and order. In fact, it should be made more obligatory than Latin in the school curriculum. We cannot follow the example of Anglo-Saxon civilization without knowing its language. Industry, he goes on to say, is the great tranquillizer. It leads mankind through prosperity and wealth to order, and through order to liberty, as is the case in England and the United States. Alberdi also rushes to the defense of the gaucho. The producers of wealth are the rural communities, "where wealth and opulence exist, and where civilization exists".[23] The services of the gaucho should be utilized,

---

[22] Juan Bautista Alberdi, *Proceso a Sarmiento* (Buenos Aires: Caldea, 1967), p. 9.
[23] Alberdi, p. 11.

stresses Alberdi. "It is necessary to civilize the gaucho instead of offending him. He who does not understand this is inept."[24]

Like Sarmiento, Alberdi sought to organize the nation's structure and economic development after the fall of the dictator Rosas in 1852. Setting forth his ideas with regard to a proper constitution for Argentina, he proposes a constitution such as that of the United States, as a possibility for his country's governmental structure, one which would insure political stability. Alberdi was opposed to a strongly centralized form of government with its seat of power in the capital. He likewise looked with disfavor upon a decentralized system which gave too much autonomy to the individual provinces. The latter case, he maintained, was akin to the Confederation of the United States of 1778, rather than the Constitution of 1787. Alberdi claimed that the first was a pure federation which almost ruined the country in eight years, while the latter was a mixed system under which the United States developed, a compromise between the two extremes of unitary and federal forms of the State. Alberdi wanted a model that could be adjusted to the needs of his country and, curiously enough, found it in the Constitution of the State of Massachusetts. Famous North Americans were his ideal. It was by way of Franklin and Robert Fulton, he maintained, that the civilization of the United States could best be introduced into Spanish America.

If Sarmiento and Alberdi stressed economic, political and social development for their country, believing that advanced capitalist nations were worthy models to be imitated, Ricardo Rojas emphasized the spiritual and collective consciousness of Argentina, based on Hispanic traditions and values, an antidote to the importation of foreign ideas. The soul of a people, Rojas asserted, was the collective memory or psychology of that people. Rojas's initial reaction to Sarmiento's "civilization versus barbarism" was couched in terms of praise of the Spanish and Indian heritages. Subsequently, he admitted the importance of other European influences which contributed to Argentine culture. What was desirable was a synthesis which would avoid the two extremes: neither barbaric nativism nor exaggerated cosmopolitanism. A healthy culture is the collective result of structuring traditions, political institutions, philosophical doctrines and emotional symbols – all of which make a nation aware of itself.[25]

Sarmiento's thesis was attacked from still another point of view. Whereas the Educator-President and his compatriot Alberdi criticized their nation's defects with a view toward improvement, Ezequiel Martínez Estrada offered a depressing commentary saturated with pessimism, of Argentina's woes: its spiritual poverty, ethical vices and a false scale of values (see Chapter 6). Especially powerful in its negative influence is the Argentine Pampa, because of the effects it exerts on the inhabitants. Solitude, fear, and suspicion

[24] Alberdi, p. 11.
[25] See in this connection Ricardo Rojas, *Eurindia* (Buenos Aires: Losada, 1951).

are their outstanding personality characteristics. We must accept this reality, maintained Martínez Estrada, and do so bravely, in order to conquer it; we should bring it to the surface of our consciousness so that it will dissipate and we can then survive in a healthier atmosphere. Meanwhile, Argentines live in a state of uncertainty and instability. "Civilization" has been imposed artificially upon a "national barbarism".[26] The dichotomy is therefore false, and accounts for the unending political chaos to which this country has been exposed.

It should be recognized that what has been hinted at all along is not slavish imitation of the North American model. Democratic principles and practices cannot be imitated mechanically by societies which are not prepared, historically and culturally, for such immediate implementation. What is important, instead, is the emphasis on the content and spirit of these principles, not necessarily the form, to be applied and developed in accordance with the circumstances of the specific cultural milieu concerned.

* * *

The activities of the United States in Spanish America both overt and covert, produced a veritable outpouring of anti-U.S. commentaries – some more vitriolic than others – dating back to the promulgation of the Monroe Doctrine. U.S. governments were attacked in print and in the public forum; U.S. society was evaluated, usually in negative fashion, and its citizens mocked for their undesirable personality traits.

In perusing the works of Spanish American writers, it is not too difficult to compile a lexicon of derogatory references. North American racism was a perennial target. Thus, for example, Juan Montalvo, of Ecuador, the implacable foe of his country's dictators, writing in the nineteenth century, stated that in the United States where democracy reigned, Blacks were barred from hotels and restaurants. The most democratic country in the world inspired terror in South Americans. "It is necessary to be blonde in order to be somebody. My face is not the type to be exhibited in New York, although I am neither zambo nor mulatto."[27]

Needless to say, New York has experienced considerable demographic change since Montalvo wrote his essay. Even though he admired the ability, strength and incredible progress of the North Americans, "their motto is atrocious. *Time is money, money is God*. I am amazed and filled with bitterness at the fact that a people, so intelligent, religious, and progressive, can vilify and oppress Mulattos and Blacks".[28] Fiction and poetry also

---

[26] Ezequiel Martínez Estrada, 5th ed. *Radiografía de la pampa* (Buenos Aires: Losada, 1961), pp. 344–46.

[27] Juan Montalvo, "La hermosura invisible", in *Carlos Ripoll, Conciencia intelectual de América* (New York: Las Américas 1966), p. 135.

[28] Montalvo, in Ripoll, p. 134.

played host to anti-U.S. sentiment. The great Nicaraguan poet, Rubén Darío, produced some of the finest vitriolic verse directed at the United States, as a result of the latter's policies in Central America. His poem "A Roosevelt" is illustrative of the Spanish American distrust of the United States. The poet echoes the fear of his fellow Spanish Americans in the face of potential imperialistic ventures by the "great and powerful North". With a fine sense of irony, he addresses Theodore Roosevelt: "You are the United States/ You are the future invader/ You are a professor of the strenuous life/ As fools say nowadays." Expressing the continent's unease at U.S. expansionism and its interest in the Panama Canal, he concludes defiantly: "And you think all is yours:/ You still lack one thing – God!"[29]

Yet Darío could also be diplomatic. When in 1904 he travelled with his country's delegation to the Pan-American Conference in Río de Janeiro, he composed "Salutación al águila". "Welcome, O Magical Eagle", he calls out to the United States, expressing the hope that the symbol, "so deeply beloved by Walt Whitman", is closely related to the condor, which represents Hispanic America. The implication is obvious: the peoples they symbolize ought to live in friendship and harmony.

The difference between the tone of this ode and that of "A Roosevelt", is almost incredible. Perhaps, suggests the critic Dundas Craig, the favorable note in "Salutación al águila" was due to the fact that Darío, the poet turned diplomat, felt he had "to say something" rather than, "something to say".[30]

Darío visited the United States in the 1890s and recorded his impressions, comparing the cities he saw with Shakespeare's Calibán (the spirit of vulgarity and utilitarianism), a symbol to be utilized subsequently by the Uruguayan essayist José Enrique Rodó. New York, in the eyes of Darío, is a monster, Chicago, the apotheosis of the pig, and Calibán is saturated with whiskey. North Americans are akin to "buffaloes with silver teeth" who shove one another in animal-like fashion, as they run through the streets in quest of the dollar.[31]

Despite this caustic criticism of United States materialism, Darío admitted that the "Colossus of the North" had produced some first-rate artists. In 1900 he admired the United States exhibit at the Paris International Exhibition, and contrasted the favorable treatment accorded writers and artists in the United States with that received by Spanish Americans in their respective countries. Even though the greater part of the population of the United States is dedicated to the worship of the dollar, he admits that there is nevertheless

29 Rubén Darío, "To Roosevelt", in G. Dundas Craig, *The Modernist Trend in Spanish-American Poetry* (Berkeley: University of California Press, 1934), pp. 69–71.

30 Craig, p. 272.

31 José Agustín Balserio, "Estudios rubendarianos: Arieles y Calibanes", *Revista Hispánica Moderna*, 31, Nos. 1–4 (Jan.–Oct. 1965), p. 47.

a minority possessed of undeniable excellence.[32] In addition to amassing huge fortunes, North Americans are also capable of lofty thoughts. "They write books, build railroads, compose poetry and launch scientific theories which the world accepts and respects."[33]

As for Spanish America fiction, the anti-Yankee motif has been a popular theme, especially in the Mexican and Central American novel, due undoubtedly to the close proximity of the United States. For example, in the early part of the present century, *La sombra de la Casa Blanca* by Máximo Soto-Hall of Guatemala dealt with the efforts of Wall Street brokers to build a canal through Nicaragua. *El problema*, by the same author, written during the Spanish American War, is probably the first anti-imperialist novel.

The Nobel Prize winner Miguel Angel Asturias aims some of his sharpest darts at Wall Street and the banana barons. With a pen dripping with vitriol, he refers to the Green Pope, personification of the United Fruit Company, who "wiggles a finger and a boat moves or stops. He says one word and a Republic is bought. He sneezes hard and a President is toppled. He scratches his rear end and a revolution erupts".[34] And elsewhere, "the President of the company, the vice-presidents, the area managers and superintendents, all faceless, but possessed of an implacable will, scurry about like blond rats...".[35]

Two Costa Rican authors should also be mentioned at this point. Joaquín Gutiérrez describes the lot of the black laborer on the U.S.-owned banana plantations. Carlos Luis Fallas in *Mamita Yunái*, does the same, but adds the indigenous element to the cast of characters. Obviously, "Yunái" refers to the United Fruit.

The Nicaraguan Hernán Robleto centered his novelistic efforts around U.S. intervention and its repercussions (*Sangre en el trópico* and *Los estranguladores*). One of Baldomero Lillo's short stories, *El grisú*, which depicts the miserable existence of the Chilean miners, features a Mr. Davis, chief engineer, who is described by the author as a despot and the personification of the "blond beast".

In *Doña Bárbara*, the Venezuelan novelist Rómulo Gallegos portrays a rapacious Yankee alcoholic, known as "Mr Danger". However, in all justice, it should be pointed out that Gallegos does not deal with all Yankees in this manner. In subsequent novels, the North American evolves from an unscrupulous, at times, infantile type, to an intelligent, fair-minded individual, e.g., Mr. Hardman in *Sobre la misma tierra*.[36]

[32]   David H. Allen, Jr. "Rubén Darío frente a la creciente influencia de los Estados Unidos", *Revista Iberoamericana*, 33, No. 64 (1967), p. 389.

[33]   Allen, p. 393.

[34]   Miguel Angel Asturias, *Viento fuerte* (Buenos Aires: Losada, 1950), p. 99.

[35]   Asturias, pp. 208–09.

[36]   Anson C. Piper, "El Yankee en las obras de Gallegos", *Hispania*, 33, No. 4 (1950), pp. 338–41.

In more recent times, the banana industry makes its appearance once more as the symbol of aggressive U.S. imperialism in the "best seller" *Cien años de soledad* by Gabriel García Márquez. On this occasion, the strike called by the workers on the banana plantations gives rise to a massacre by the military in collusion with the company.

Many additional examples of anti-United States expression in prose and poetry can be listed to demonstrate further the considerable extent to which this sentiment can be found. The Chilean poetess, Gabriela Mistral, winner of the Nobel Prize, exclaims: "Help us to conquer or at least stop the invasion...by blond America that wants to sell everything to us, to populate our fields and cities with lots of machinery, factories, even those things we have but don't know how to exploit..."[37] Gabriela Mistral's compatriot Pablo Neruda, another Nobel Prize winner, also aims his sharpest darts at the United Fruit Company in his poem which carries that title. Beside Ford Motors, Anaconda, and Coca Cola, Inc., The United Fruit "reserved for itself the heartland/ and coast of my country/ the delectable waist of America".[38]

Still another example is provided by Juan José Arévalo, in his controversial study, *The Shark and the Sardines*.[39] Arévalo, a former president of Guatemala, maintains that the United States, at one time representative of the spirit of democracy, is now characterized by greed and ruthlessness. The shark, of course, represents the powerful nation to the North. Any contract entered into by the shark and the sardines is, of course, not only ludicrous, but fatal.

The hostility evinced toward the United States is expressed succinctly by the Argentine Manuel Ugarte, whose comments must be placed within the framework of his reaction to the Monroe Doctrine: "Naturally, the United States has been interested in preserving the hegemony and protection which allows it to prepare and assure its continual penetration, its future expansion and domination of America...The United States defends us against Europe, but who will defend us against the United States?"[40] And finally, the defiant challenge hurled at the "blond beasts" by Augusto César Sandino, the guerrilla leader who fought against American marines in his native Nicaragua in the 1920s: "The blond beasts...avidly observe our political and economic moves...The Yankees know us well and take advantage of our cultural condition and the flippancy of our nature in order to endanger us if this should suit

---

[37] Quoted in Victor M. Valenzuela, *Anti-United States Sentiment in Latin American Literature and Other Essays* (Bethlehem, Pa.: Lehigh University, 1982), p. 47.

[38] Valenzuela, p. 54.

[39] Juan José Arévalo, *The Shark and the Sardines*. Translated from the Spanish by Jane Cobb and Raúl Osegueda (New York: L. Stuart, 1961); original title: *Fábula del Tiburón y las Sardinas*.

[40] Carlos M. Rama, *La imagen de los Estados Unidos en la América Latina* (México: Sep Diana, 1975), p. 111.

their interests...The Yankees are the worst enemies of our people...Speaking
of the Monroe Doctrine, they state: America for the Americans...I shall
modify the statement as follows: The United States of North America for the
Yankees; Latin America for the Indo-Latins...The Yankees can come to our
Latin America as guests, but never as masters..."[41]

* * *

The classic criticism of the United States by a Spanish American was
made by José Enrique Rodó at the turn of the century. Although he had his
precursors, his work was a reaction to the overemphasis of the positivist
point of view and glorification of material and utilitarian values. The admirers and would-be imitators of the United States had, since Sarmiento and
Alberdi, argued too long and too hard. Rodó's *Ariel* could be considered a
reply to Sarmiento in the sense that it proposed "disinterested Latinism" as a
counterweight to the Argentine's admiration for the economic pragmatism of
the United States. In short, Rodó's message to the youth of the continent
aspired to be the symbol of Hispanic American humanism and idealism,
represented by Ariel, the adversary of United States materialism, namely,
Calibán. In Rodó's view, Calibán, personification of sensuality, vulgarity
and mediocrity, was threatening to engulf Spanish America.

Rodó's thesis suggests that the Latin American ideal be equated with that
of ancient Athens. The Spanish American should aspire to achieve the harmonious development of his personality, as did the Athenian, the free citizen
who maintained all of his faculties – physical, mental, and spiritual – in
perfect equilibrium. Rodó did not mention the fact that the free man's
enjoyment of leisure was only made possible by the existence of a social
order, the major portion of which was composed of slaves.

No one component of the individual's personality should be emphasized
to the exclusion of the others, as is the case of the North American who is
interested only in material well-being. The Yankee, claims Rodó, represents
utilitarian values; the Spanish American, by contrast, aspires to the realization of the higher moral and spiritual ideals.

The principal theme discussed in *Ariel* is the relationship between culture
and democracy. Interestingly enough, of the six selections which comprise
the volume, only one deals with the cultural model offered by the United
States. Rodó, who had never visited the United States, seemed to anticipate
the anti-Yankee reaction provoked by the publication of his book, and attempted, apparently in vain, to dispel it.[42] Yet despite his efforts, Spanish
American youth acclaimed what it perceived as an anti-U.S. message. Ariel

---

[41] Rama, p. 211.
[42] Emir Rodríguez Monegal, "Las metamorfosis de Calibán", *Vuelta* (México), 3, No. 25
(1978), p. 24.

and Arielism became the humanistic justification for the animosity felt toward "Yankee imperialism". The opposition to the "dollar diplomacy" of the United States could now clothe itself in cultural trappings. At this moment in history – the United States had just won its war against Spain – Spanish Americans needed some measure of psychological comfort and resorted to a defense mechanism expressed as follows: "You, North Americans may have your material and military power, but we have our humanism and spirituality."

The basic error, of course, characteristic of this thesis, was contained in the premise that democracy as practised in the United States, was represented by the spirit of utilitarianism and mediocrity. What civilization gained in extension, it lost in depth. A closer examination of Rodó's hypothesis would lead one to conclude that there can be no disagreement with his contention that equality is not synonymous with equality of opportunity. All members of society have the same right to aspire to moral superiority; society, in the form of the state, has the duty to see to it that all of its members are so placed as to be able to seek and attain their highest level. Thus each human superiority, wherever it exists, must be brought to light. After the initial equality is granted, any resultant inequality cannot be frowned upon, since it is due to natural differences in human beings. Paradoxical though it may seem, equality of opportunity results in inequality of achievement. Such was the type of democracy favored by Rodó, and although it might have surprised him, by Thomas Jefferson as well.

The idea of a dichotomy between a utilitarian United States and an esthetic Spanish America is no longer so widespread, although Rodó still strikes a sympathetic note. Rodó himself wished to put an end to the Ariel-Calibán polarity by suggesting that Calibán could be placed at the service of Ariel and guided properly. Since World War II, the Ariel-Calibán antinomy has lost ground, and has been replaced by more sophisticated argumentation. It cannot be denied that there are many Ariels in the United States, and an impressive number of Calibáns in Latin America.[43] In short, the old Ariel-Calibán dichotomy is no longer valid, i.e., if it ever was. If North American material values are penetrating Latin America, then one may venture the suggestion that this is what Latin America wants. It is too easy to say that Calibán is the enemy emanating from the United States. Let Spanish America look inside itself and behold Calibán within, that self-same Calibán that cooperates with all other Calibáns from other countries.[44]

Furthermore, one may add the following demurrer: in asserting the humanism of the Spanish American and the materialism of his northern neighbor,

[43] John T. Reid, The Rise and Decline of the Ariel-Calibán Antithesis in Spanish America", *The Americas*, 34, No. 3 (1978), pp. 345–55.

[44] Waldo Frank, *Primer mensaje a la América Hispana* (Madrid: Revista de Occidente, 1929), pp. 280–81.

are we comparing two equivalent groups? How valid and reliable are the samples? Are we juxtaposing the elitist intellectual of Latin America and the "Archie Bunker" type of the United States? It would be just as ludicrous to place alongside each other, for purposes of comparison, scientists and philosophers of the North American universities on the one hand, and the landless peasants of Mexico or Peru, on the other .

Finally, an interesting revision of symbolic values has been suggested by the Cuban Fernández Retamar. Taking his cue from the writings of the Argentine socialist Aníbal Ponce, and inspired by anti-colonialist Caribbean writers (e.g., George Lamming, Aimé Césaire and Edmund Brathwaite), Fernández Retamar has reinterpreted the meaning and role of Calibán and Ariel. Calibán linked derisively with "canibal", no longer represents the brutish, anti-humanist spirit of the United States. He symbolizes, instead, the downtrodden people of Latin America who wage war against foreign (U.S.) imperialistic interests, represented by Shakespeare's Próspero. Furthermore, Ariel is not the antagonist of Calibán, as argued by Rodó, but rather the Latin American intellectual who, together with Calibán, will resist the common enemy, Próspero. In the course of their joint struggle, they will help each other and forge a bond which will redound to their mutual benefit.[45]

The Mexican philosopher José Vasconcelos follows in the footsteps of Rodó. He chastises the Spanish Americans for their imitation of the United States. Even Latin American pragmatism is inferior to that of the North Americans. At least the latter have developed their practice into a systematic philosophy. Vasconcelos urges Spanish Americans to enrich their cultural roots, rather than imitate the technology of the United States. Repeating the oft-quoted refrain, he asserts that the latter has made tremendous strides in the utilization of the machine, but in the process it has sacrificed spiritual values.

Vasconcelos is one of many who cannot resist the temptation to indulge in stereotyped labels as he characterizes the inhabitants of the two Americas. These utterances now retain a quaint flavor and are only of historical interest, especially in view of the profound demographic changes which have taken place in both Americas. Thus, in Vasconcelos's judgment, the North American is hard-working; the Spanish American is indolent. Even philosophers are not immune to facile generalizations. The "workaholic" of the North sticks to his work until it is finished. His Spanish-American counterpart compensates for his fickleness and laziness by being superior in mental agility.[46] For the native of the United States life is a series of tasks to be performed. For his Southern neighbor, life is a series of joyous parties. Or to

[45] Roberto Fernández Retamar, *Calibán cannibale* (Paris: François Maspero, 1973), pp. 42–52.

[46] I. Bar-Lewaw Mulstock, *José Vasconcelos. Vida y Obra* (México: Clásica Selecta Editora Librería, 1965), p. 108.

put it differently: the former has to work hard even at playing, for the latter, work is play. This is stereotyped thinking at its worst.

Vasconcelos, Minister of Education following the Mexican Revolution, was particularly interested in educational values. Culture patterns and value systems were, naturally, interrelated with educational philosophy. The school system in the United States, he maintained, placed too much emphasis on the practical and the useful. This was especially undesirable at the higher level of education, where specialization was emphasized. According to Vasconcelos, specialization appeals to the empirical temperament of the North American and should be balanced by a greater stress on spiritual values. The latter emphasis is more in keeping with the Spanish American mind.

The Anglo-Saxon type of education, Vasconcelos continues, is symbolized by the figure of Robinson Crusoe on a desert island, who is faced by a continuous need to solve problems and invent what is useful in order to survive. On the other hand, the Latin American type of education identifies with another figure, that of Ulysses, which represents perpetual inquiry and endless weaving of dreams. The North American is interested in the *how* of things; his distinguishing characteristic is problem solving. The Spanish American is always asking *why*, thereby revealing a philosophical bent; again simplistic practicality versus humanistic idealism, or in the language of Vasconcelos, "robinsonismo" versus "odiseísmo".

Two other terms, suggested by the Mexican philosopher, ought to be mentioned, the meaning of which should be obvious: "Bolivarismo" and "Monroísmo". The former indicates the longed-for federation of all the Spanish American republics, an ideal to which the great Liberator had aspired, and one which would achieve political and spiritual unity. Opposed to "Bolivarismo" is "Monroísmo", a derivation of United States foreign policy, manifested in concrete form by the doctrine of Pan Americanism (to evolve subsequently into the Organization of American States), which seeks to maintain control of the Hispanic nations to the South. In this connection, Vasconcelos charged that United States Protestantism was making inroads in Latin America and sowing discord among its inhabitants. Protestantism was an ally of U.S. capitalism, the right arm of "Monroísmo", and therefore inimical to Spanish American values.

Vasconcelos perceived the two Americas as two distinct civilizations: one prefers the exclusive predominance of the white man; the other is the scenario for the formation of a new race, an ethnic mix or "raza cósmica", which would combine all the spiritual elements of the other races in one grand synthesis. The "cosmic race" would act as an antidote to the deleterious effects of old nationalistic creeds. It would be a racial and cultural amalgam of diverse elements, and would ultimately produce a new and improved human type. Of course, Vasconcelos's assumption is an optimistic one. It can be argued that another equally valid premise may be advanced, namely one which speaks in terms of the possible union of negative characteristics of the different racial groups. What sort of Utopia would result in that case?

In later years, Vasconcelos, somewhat mellowed, was more kindly disposed toward the United States. He admitted that Pan-American Congresses were accomplishing some positive results, e.g., scholarships for study in the United States. Seeming to execute a complete about-face, he asserted that North Americans were the most idealistic people of the time. He was willing to accept the example of the United States in questions of governmental systems, and affirmed that only democracy could be an effective form of government for Spanish America. Even in his *Indología* which is representative of his anti-U.S. stance, he expressed the hope that men of good will in both Americas could continue the struggle against imperialism.[47]

Contrary to what Rodó advocated, his compatriot, Alberto Zum Felde, maintained that Spanish America should understand that certain influences emanating from the United States would be of decided benefit because they would aid in the correction of certain defects without necessarily altering Spanish American "essence". Rodó's famous reference to the United States ("I admire them but I do not love them") is symptomatic of an attitude which can and should be modified. One can love in the sense of projecting sympathy even for those who are radically different.[48]

The contrast between the two value systems, represented respectively by the United States and Spanish America, is expressed graciously by Zum Felde. The North American, he believes, possesses practical sense, but to an excessive degree; he is also woefully deficient in the poetic component of his soul. On the other hand, the Spanish American is overflowing as far as the poetic factor is concerned, but his practical sense is lamentably inadequate. What is needed, Zum Felde goes on to say, is a measure of cross-fertilization. "Let us inject a small amount of lyricism in the North American and a few drops of practicality in his Spanish American neighbor, but only a few drops!" One can almost detect a mischievous twinkle in Zum Felde's eyes as he wrote this.[49]

The well-worn contrasts continue to be repeated: The Spanish American is passionate, doctrinaire and contemplative; the Anglo-American is dispassionate, pragmatic and realistic. The former is often intransigent whereas the latter tends to be conciliatory. The man of the north engages in expansionist activities; he is characteristically optimistic.[50] Hence, North and South have their corresponding equivalents in the following antithetical

[47] José Vasconcelos, *Indología, una interpretación de la cultura iberoamericana* (Paris: Agencia Mundial de Librería, 1926), p. 197.

[48] Guillermo Díaz-Plaja, *Hispanoamérica en su literatura* (Navarra: Salvat 1972), p. 172.

[49] Alberto Zum Felde, *El problema de la cultura en América* (Buenos Aires: Losada, 1943), p. 115.

[50] Edmund Stephen Urbanski, *Hispanoamérica, sus razas y civilizaciones* (New York: Eliseo Torres & Sons, 1972), pp. 199–200.

concepts: authoritarian idealism versus pragmatic liberalism; technological expertise versus abstract speculation.

Another opponent of Rodó's point of view is the Chilean thinker, Enrique Molina. Molina rejects the Uruguayan's assertion that the United States has progressed only in the material sense, and that Spanish America should be the repository of all that is humanistic and spiritual. The United States, protests Molina, can also boast of philosophers, novelists, playwrights, poets and artists.

As for exploitation of Spanish America by foreign interests, Molina seems to rebuke his own fellow Spanish Americans. Let us not complain about others who exploit our natural resources, he writes, if we are not prepared to exploit them ourselves. We should improve our efficiency, our means of production, our general potential and eradicate the defects from which we suffer.[51]

Molina offers additional insight into the differences which characterized the colonization of the two Americas. The North American, he claims, struck roots in a limited geographical area, and spread out only after Independence had been achieved and the colonies united. In contrast, the Spaniards settled over the length and breadth of the entire continent, and only afterward did they wage a war for independence. The enormity of the land mass which they populated made separation and disunity inevitable.

Eugenio María de Hostos, the Puerto Rican thinker, also reflected upon the significance of the discovery of America. America, for Hostos, appears to be a geographical entity which will serve as a haven for the millions of Europeans, a political system based on the guaranteed equality of individual rights, and a society which will assure religious peace; in short, a continent brimming over with possibilities for a new civilization.[52]

In this connection. Hostos compares the evolution of the two Americas beginning with the colonial period. Whereas the America of the North adhered to a philosophy of critical examination of ideas which led to the practice of religious freedom, the Spanish American colonists followed in the footsteps of the religious counter-revolution under the watchful eye of the Inquisition. Moreover, the English colonies embarked upon the road to representative democracy, "the loftiest political conception and the most powerful legal system arrived at by man; the Spanish colonies, by contrast, freed themselves from an inefficient mother country only to become dependent upon political errors, inherited from colonialism".[53]

Hostos cannot be too harsh in his comparison of the two Americas. In

---

51 Enrique Molina, *Confesión filosófica y llamado de superación a la América Hispana* (Santiago: Nascimento, 1942), p. 103.

52 Eugenio María de Hostos, *Obras completas, La Cuna de América* (Havana: Cultural 1939), 1, pp. 38–39.

53 Hostos in Ripoll, "El Día de América", p. 151.

order to effect a fair evaluation, one must take into account the differences
between their respective colonial systems. Which of the two Americas, he
asks, had more difficulties to overcome? What sort of immigrant had arrived
in each, and what role did he play in its development? Only after these
questions are answered will one understand why the United States has made
such phenomenal progress, and why there is such a gap between the two
Americas. Yet even though he expresses his admiration for the United States,
its strength and political institutions, its common sense, rational development, confidence in itself and in the future, he nevertheless questions its
ability to be a prudent mentor and leader of other nations of the New
World.[54]

In this article, too, he expresses his utter amazement at what the United
States has achieved in the course of the first century of its existence, with
special emphasis on its military and industrial accomplishments. What im-
presses him particularly is the fusion, in harmonious fashion, of the different
ethnic groups, e.g., the Yankee, Irish, German, Scandinavian, Swiss, etc.,
which has resulted in the creation of the loyal soldier, who, in turn, exem-
plifies the wholesome American citizen.[55]

Of course, this was written against the background of the Civil War which
had been concluded a decade earlier. It is at this point that he chastises
Europe which had indulged in monarchist slander against the Republic.
Europeans, steeped in monarchical traditions, had charged disdainfully that
the United States was a society of galley slaves. Hostos reproaches Europe
for having engaged in a campaign of calumny against Spanish America.
What gives Europe the right, he asks, to send its warships to Montevideo
every time foreigners believe their interests threatened in that part of the
world? In another essay, he includes the United States as well in his criticism. He condemns the practice of dispatching marines to Panama every
time a revolt breaks out in that country.[56]

Hostos asserts indignantly that European societies required fifteen centuries to create a spirit of nationality. With what right, then, do they expect
the Spanish American countries to create a spirit of nationality in less than a
century of political independence? Europe has gone through nineteen centuries of wars and revolutions. In all this time, it has been victimized by
ignorance and barbarism which it has not yet succeeded in eliminating. How,
then, can Europe dare to expect Latin America to work and progress with the
meager educational resources at its disposal?

Hostos, then, insists on the need for a greater measure of comprehension

[54] Eugenio María de Hostos, *Obras completas, España y América* (Paris: Ediciones
Literarias y Artísticas, 1954), 21, p. 324.

[55] Hostos, *España y América*, p. 322.

[56] Hostos, *Obras completas, Temas sudamericanos* (Havana: Cultural S.A., 1939), 7, p.
215.

of the Spanish American problem, recognizing at the same time that there are defects and shortcomings which must be remedied. He strikes a familiar note: Spanish America must encourage immigration, combat ignorance and fanaticism, and above all, educate. This is the road to civilization, to universality.

* * *

Peru's well-known firebrand, Manuel González Prada, is one of those who come to the defense of the United States. His vitriolic attitude toward Spain and her colonial heritage is sufficient motivation to cause him to aim some of his most satirical darts at those Spaniards who believe that the Yankees are nothing more than sausage vendors and hog butchers. Given his interest in science and industrial progress, he assails those who are blind to the material accomplishments realized in the United States: the construction of highways, bridges, canals and railroads. Yet he is also the humanist who sneers at those who would deny that the North Americans have achieved prominence in the intellectual world. The United States "possesses museums, libraries and universities, equal and superior to those of the Old World".[57] And in what appears to be a final burst of extreme exasperation, he exclaims: "Poor Spanish America is destined to return to a state of barbarism unless the United States performs an immediate service, namely, conquering it."[58]

At times, admiration and rejection of the "Colossus of the North" characterize the comments made by the same Spanish American thinker, as in the case of Justo Sierra, Mexican historian and educator. Strongly influenced by positivist currents, he viewed the future progress of his country in terms of economic and educational development. The more civilized nations were those with more schools, railroads and telegraph facilities. He was probably thinking of the United States when he suggested that railroads and factories link nations with one another. Yet there is also fear that can be detected in the following passage: "If we do not preserve our own identity through our own efforts, the Mexican plant will disappear in the shadow of others, infinitely more vigorous."[59]

In 1895 Sierra visited the United States in order to observe those "more vigorous" plants. Despite the fact that, by his own admission, he was not at home in English, he has left us with some of his impressions, quite amusing and not unlike many stereotypes which foreign visitors have contributed to the world of travel literature. He writes, for example: "If I were to depict

---

57 Manuel González Prada, "Españoles y Yankees", in Ripoll, p. 207.
58 González Prada, in Leopoldo Zea, *Precursores del pensamiento latinamericano contemporáneo* (México: Sep Diana, 1979), p. 28.
59 Justo Sierra, "Epistolario y papeles privados", in *Obras completas* (México: UNAM, 1977), 14, p. 356.

these people, I would describe them in the form of an athlete...They are marvellously developed: neck, arms, thighs, back and torso...And the face? Characterized by granite-like eyes and iron jaws, due to an insatiable appetite...The women want to be like men, to partake also of the struggle for life, i.e., for luxury...scrambling by means of matrimony and divorce...in search of happiness...but without a soul. Good-bye, land of the unexpected, the colossal and the stupendous; you were born yesterday and you have grown in an hour."[60]

The theme is further developed by Pedro Henríquez Ureña who affirms that the first Utopia to be realized on the earth was the establishment of the United States. This is an undeniable fact, he asserts, which must be recognized, but unfortunately, having been born in freedom, "after having been the shield for the victims of all tyranny, and the mirror for all the apostles of the democratic ideal...this gigantic country became wealthy and lost its head: the material devoured the spiritual...The nation which was the archetype of liberty is today one of the least free countries in the world."[61] Should we permit our America, he asks, to follow a similar path? His reply is emphatic. If Spanish America is to be but an extension of Europe, if we do not decide that it should be the land of promise for humanity, then there is no justification for us.[62]

* * *

The pendulum continues to oscillate as the decades go by and we arrive at the contemporary period.

The Colombian Germán Arciniegas has performed a dual function in his rich and varied career. A leading spokesman for democracy, he has not only interpreted his continent to the North American students, but also presented the United States and its problems to Spanish Americans. His essay *Este pueblo de América* is an attempt to improve upon historical accounts which are, in his eyes, characterized by their superficiality. In the past, he claims, historians have too often been content to limit themselves to a narration of political facts. Arciniegas seeks to achieve depth, to delve beneath the mask and examine the face and expression of the soul of a people. Who is discovering whom? he asks in his discussion of the Conquest. Certainly the Spaniard did not discover the Indian. He never understood him; instead, he enslaved him. He even doubted whether he had a soul, as illustrated by the polemics between Juan Ginés de Sepúlveda and Bartolomé de las Casas. For the Spaniard, the Indian was just an animal to be exploited. The Indian was taciturn, enigmatic and difficult to penetrate. On the other hand, it seemed

60 Sierra, "Viajes en tierra", in *Obras completas*, 6, p. 192.
61 Pedro Henríquez Ureña, *La Utopía de América* (Caracas: Biblioteca Ayacucho, 1978), p. 19.
62 Henríquez Ureña, p. 11.

much easier for the Indian to "discover" the Spaniard, since the latter spoke freely and hid nothing. Arcinieagas compares the colonizing process that characterized the two Americas. In Spanish America, the Conquest preceded the colonization, whereas in the North, the colony was established first. The Conquest was still to come.

With reference to the United States, Arciniegas's portrayal of that nation is a highly favorable one. When Abraham Lincoln defined democracy in its most concrete terms as "government of the people, by the people and for the people", he crystallized an ideal for which the citizens of the United States will continue to fight endlessly, since, in Arciniegas's view, the perfect democracy still does not exist. Yet, this is precisely the function served by the concept. As long as democracy is an ideal, still to be attained, America will continue to have some meaning in the world.[63]

This point should be emphasized. Large segments of the world's population wish to behold the America of Lincoln, i.e., the optimistic and democratic America, the "athletic democracy" of Walt Whitman. The democratic traditions of the United States have a long history. They can be made meaningful if applied to changing circumstances. Other peoples of the world have had to experience violent revolution in order to establish democracy. The United States has only to extend and carry out its democratic traditions and not suspend or ignore them.

Jesús Arango Cano, another contemporary Colombian writer, attempts to present a composite picture of the average North American in as objective a manner as is humanly possible, based on his eight-year sojourn in the United States as a university student.

Generally speaking, writes Arango Cano, the American is a hard-working, generous worker, an excellent friend and affectionate parent. This strongly contradicts the negative impression he creates abroad in the role of tourist or business man, namely, an individual who is rude, boastful and egotistical. In his social relations, maintains Arango, the American is jovial, but somewhat naive; he is prone to occupy himself with the simplest of pastimes, especially when he travels abroad. How is this apparently infantile behavior to be explained? According to Arango, the explanation is to be found in the excessive technological mechanization of life in the United States. Routine and monotony characterize an individual's job, whether in the factory or in the office, to such extent that life has become depersonalized. In short, man has become an automaton.[64]

At the end of the working day, the average American is so fatigued as a result of the boring and tedious nature of his work, that he seeks out the

[63] Germán Arciniegas, *Este pueblo de América* (México: Fondo de Cultura Económica, 1945), pp. 167–81.
[64] Jesús Arango Cano, *Estados Unidos, Mito y Realidad* (Bogotá: LIbrería Voluntad, 1959), p. 82.

simplest types of diversion for the purpose of relaxation. No theatre, no lectures, no "heavy" reading; T.V. entertainment of the lightest variety will suffice. This accounts for the infantile tastes which are developed and reflected in his behavior. It also serves to explain the "infantilism" of the "ugly" American when he finds himself in a foreign country: his boisterous carrying on, his exaggerated apparel and occasional drunken brawls – all in the name of relaxation", of "getting away from it all". The inhabitants of the Spanish American host country will gladly accept his American dollars, but will view his behavior with a good deal of amusement and, at times, resentment.[65]

These are, regrettably, the impressions of an educated Spanish American who, nevertheless, is careful to point out that one should avoid generalizations. There are many Americans who do not fit into the above mentioned category.

Many Spanish Americans feel that the visitor from the United States exhibits a superiority complex. Perhaps this may be due to the fact that he is compensating for a feeling of insecurity; he is not sure of himself when he finds himself on unfamiliar ground, facing a foreign language and culture. His so-called "superiority complex" may simply be a protective device to conceal a feeling of uncertainty and inadequacy. Then, too, it is unfortunate that at times it is the "wrong" kind of American who travels and creates these negative impressions. Regrettably, as is so often the case, those who can afford to travel, shouldn't and those who should, are unable to do so.

Arango widens his analysis of the North American personality to include some comments relative to the foreign policy of the United States and the attitude evinced by Spanish Americans as a result. The frequent reference to U.S. imperialism and military intervention is charged with resentment and hostility. However, Arango goes to great lengths to stress the distinction between the government and the people of the United States. The opposition to United States foreign policy should not detract from the respect in which the American people as a whole are held, and the admiration felt for the democratic principles upon which the nation was founded.

The Mexican philosopher Leopoldo Zea, in his critical evaluation of the United States, distinguishes between two concepts: "society" and "community". In the former, every individual seeks out elements which will make for improvement in his daily existence. In the "community", by contrast, individuals share common experiences in interconnected fashion, guided by a common purpose which transcends their particularities. According to Zea, "society" which allows for the release of individual energy tends to give free rein to egotistic drives and thus is inimical to the concept of community. For Zea, the modern era, of which the United States is the representative par

[65] Arango Cano, p. 84.

excellence, combines within itself the seeds of destruction of collective organisms which are then replaced by masses of separate individuals.[66]

Zea maintains that the essence of United States imperialism is pure unabashed greed. The ideals of the North American creed, embodied in the principles of "life, liberty and the pursuit of happiness", are universal in nature. They belong to the world, but according to Zea, the policy of United States imperialism has been to deny the opportunity to other peoples to achieve these ideals.[67] For example, his own country, he claims, has been used as "raw material" by the United States as a means for advancing North American interests.

The Mexican philosopher believes that the United States has betrayed its ideals. Freedom is being curtailed and creativity is diminishing. Western man, as exemplified by the North American, has become dehumanized; he has become a tool of the very instruments he has fashioned. The United States has its focus on the present and is striving to hold on to what has been achieved. By contrast, the Spanish American perspective is oriented toward the future and that which is yet to be attained.

The Western World has had no desire to recognize in other peoples the values which it has claimed for itself. Values such as human dignity, freedom, progress, industrialism and material comfort – all of these enjoyed by western Europe and the United States – are denied to non-Western nations. In short, what has resulted is that the West seems to be fighting against the universalization of its own culture!

Zea's compatriot, the historian Daniel Cosío Villegas, maintains that the Yankees are victims of the "quantitative" mania, i.e., they measure progress in terms of numbers. They are addicted to statistics: the volume and value of production, of exports and imports, the size of the student population, the number of patients per hospital, the proportion of telephones, automobiles and television sets relative to the population, etc.

Cosío Villegas warns his countrymen not to adopt a foreign model – in this case, the United States – with which to measure their achievements, but to follow native culture patterns. Progress is not to be evaluated solely in material terms. Human relationships should determine the degree of progress attained.

Cosío Villegas finds that Spanish American society is more rigid than that of the United States, Opportunities for economic advancement are far fewer in Spanish America. Social mobility in the North is much more fluid, an assertion which would be challenged by significant sectors in the United States. Cosío Villegas appears to sum up his contention in somewhat

---

66 Michael A. Weinstein, "Lamento y Utopía: Respuestas al Imperio Norteamericano en George Grant y Leopoldo Zea", *Nuestra América* (México, UNAM), 3, No. 8 (1983), pp. 149–50.

67 Michael A. Weinstein, p. 151.

humorous and considerably exaggerated fashion: "The daily history of the United States is replete with bootblacks or newsboys who become magnates; in our countries a comparable case would be that of a demagogue or highway robber who takes over the government overnight."[68]

The ambivalent attitudes toward the United States, characteristic of Mexico, the result of different historical circumstances, can be extended to all of Spanish America. If, after Independence, programs of social and political reform had been proposed, looking to the United States as a model in an attempt to modernize the new republics, in the present century by contrast left-wing parties together with their allies in the "theology of liberation" movement have viewed United States imperialism as the incarnation of the anti-Christ.

It has already been suggested that rapprochement versus alienation, as these affect the two Americas, has always been of concern to a considerable body of thinkers. Each point of view has had its advocates. Some have been more optimistic and hopeful than others. Octavio Paz belongs to the camp of the pessimists. He does not believe that the culture of the two Americas can be reconciled. Two competing forces, he claims, have always been present in the psyche of the Spanish American. Admiration for the originality and might of North American culture has always vied with fear and anger at the repeated intervention of the United States in the life of the Southern continent. "Latin America and Anglo-Saxon America represent two different and probably irreconcilable versions of Western civilization."[69]

With lyrical exuberance Paz offers some of his impressions of the North American personality, attitudes and institutions, contrasting them with those of the Mexican. The North American, he observes, is a reformer, not a radical, i.e., he prefers to improve procedures rather than uproot structures. He wants to use reality rather than know it. For example, he has no desire to understand death, and therefore avoids the subject. The Mexican, on the other hand, has developed a cult of death, linked to "masochistic tendencies", as well as "a certain variety of religious emotion".[70] At the same time, although aware of the danger of stereotyping and speaking of the Mexican as though he were a homogeneous, undifferentiated entity, Paz believes that only a small group of his compatriots considers itself Mexican. Mexico is the home of "a number of races speaking different languages and living on different historical levels".[71]

The North American, Paz continues, is credulous; he loves fairy tales and

---

[68] Daniel Cosío Villegas, "Los problemas de América", in José Luis Martínez, *El ensayo mexicano moderno* (México: Fondo de Cultura Económica, 1958), 1, p. 483.

[69] Luis Leal, "A Spanish American Perspective of Anglo-American Literature", *Revista Canadiense de Estudios Hispánicos* (Toronto), 5, No. 1 (1980), pp. 69–70.

[70] Octavio Paz, *The Labyrinth of Solitude*, Trans. by Lysander Kemp (New York: Grove Press, 1961), p. 23.

[71] *The Labyrinth...*, p. 11.

detective stories. He gets drunk in order to forget, whereas the Mexican does the same in order to confess. The North American is optimistic and trusting. He is an activist and believes in hygiene, health and hard work. He is also subject to a process of adaptation to his environment by means of constant repetition, issued by the media, the schools and the church.

One may well ask at this point: what society does not make use of certain techniques in order to insure that its members, from childhood on, find a proper niche for themselves, and thus guard against social disorganization? Paz's poetic language is persuasive, yet one must always guard against facile generalizations.

Paz believes that the United States is a society that wants to realize its ideals. The North American is confident of surviving, no matter how dark the future may seem, although with the advent of nuclear weapons he may appear less optimistic. Curiously enough, the North American's faith in the essential goodness of life, according to Paz, is not to be found in recent examples of literature. In this respect, Paz does not differ from many other Spanish Americans. Rodó, for example, had stated that in the United States, literature and the fine arts are the product of individuals who are alienated from their society.[72] Pedro Henríquez Ureña wanted to know why life in the United States was unsatisfactory for men and women who labor in the realm of ideas. In the United States of 1920, the thinkers and artists were rebels. That nation owes its moral and intellectual salvation to rebels like Waldo Frank, Sherwood Anderson and Theodore Dreiser. United States writers today seem to receive more favorable acclaim in Latin America to the degree that they are critical of their own country. In this connection, both Octavio Paz and Carlos Fuentes coincide in the belief that the writer's most important task is to criticize his own society. It is this critical tradition, shared by writers of both Americas, which can, perhaps, bring the nations of the new world closer to one another.

In another essay, Octavio Paz writes that for most Mexicans, the United States had always been an image before it became a reality, a conflictive duality representing a foreign object "on the other side", yet deeply imbedded in the national consciousness. Mexicans are constantly aware of the giant's shadow to the North, even when they choose to ignore it. The giant can appear as a good-natured simpleton as well as a dangerous monster.[73]

The concept of time and temporal perspective is also worthy of comment in this connection. Psychologically, the historical perspective of the two Americas seem to be pointed in opposite directions. For example, Latin America prefers a traditional orientation rooted in the past and chooses to live in the present, whereas the United States continually projects toward the

72 Luis Leal, p. 66.
73 Octavio Paz, "El espejo indiscreto", in *El ogro filantrópico* (México: Joaquín Mortiz, 1979), p. 53.

future.[74] These contrasting positions are intimately associated with the way in which time is viewed, undoubtedly a result of conditioning by the type of economic organization which prevails. For example, from a linguistic standpoint, the contrast is illustrated by the oft-quoted difference between the English phrase "My watch runs" and the Spanish equivalent, "My watch walks" (mi reloj anda).

With regard to the above, an additional commentary is offered by Juan Roura Parella, a Spanish professor who taught in the United States and who is, therefore, in a position to reflect on the question in comparative fashion, often in a humorous vein. For example, time ceases to exist when the Spanish American takes his "siesta"; all cares and preoccupations are put aside temporarily. On the other hand, in the United States the average businessman, to cite a concrete case, continues to be concerned with his affairs at the office even during his lunch hour. This would explain the on-going practice of the "business lunch". The clock continues to tick after he rushes back to the office. Time is no longer a fluid affair, as in the case of the Spanish American who allows it to course through his entire being while he relaxes, but, rather a formidable opponent to be faced and contended with, a concrete, demanding master.

Roura Parella continues his observations, often bordering on questionable generalizations. For example, economic and utilitarian values predominate in the North; love and friendship in the south. "Latin America is the land of love, religion and adventure... in the man of the South sex is interwoven with other superior forms of love, whereas in the North it is a physiological function, akin to the satisfaction of hunger..."[75]

The reference to love and sex brings to mind Count Hermann Keyserling's commentaries on Latin American men and women. His impressions, gathered as a result of his travels, leave no doubt as to his overwhelming attachment to the Latin American landscape. Nevertheless, he has left behind some rather choice bits. For example, with reference to Argentine males, he writes: "Sexual potency means more to the Argentines than to any other men on earth. Their life is adjusted to sensual satisfaction and procreation in a way unlike any other type of man I have ever known."[76]

His reference to women is even more entertaining. Speaking of Argentine women, he states: "In their heart of hearts they desire to be violated; they want to be able to remain entirely passive, completely irresponsible; and the sexual success South American men so frequently have in Europe is due to the fact that, despite their delicacy, they violate as a matter of course."[77] And

[74]   Paz, The contrast is suggested by Juan Roura Parella and is quoted in José Luis Abellán, *La idea de América: origen y evolución* (Madrid: Istmo, 1972), p. 52.
[75]   Quoted in Abellán, pp. 52–53.
[76]   Hermann Keyserling, *South American Meditations* (New York: Harper, 1932).
[77]   Hermann Keyserling, p. 30.

elsewhere, again with respect to women: "No woman on earth makes such masterly use of all the possibilities of passivity and deceit. None has so spider-like a way of catching a man in her net...Once an Argentine woman went so far as to tell me : 'With us, faithfulness is a disease.'...I do not in the least dispute the high qualities and, most of all, the possibilities of the South American woman; what I have said merely goes to prove her primordial womanhood, which makes her particularly seductive."[78]

In view of the above, it is refreshing to come upon more balanced judgments concerning so-called national characteristics and cross-cultural attitudes. For example, the Mexican Luis Quintanilla, in referring to Rodó, rejects the latter's allegation concerning the North American's cultural inferiority. In an effort to lay that ghost to rest, Quintanilla writes: "I believe that nothing has been more detrimental to mutual understanding in the Americas than the continental prejudice, according to which all spiritual culture belongs to Latin America and all material civilization to the United States."[79]

Finally, Luis Alberto Sánchez compares the two Americas with reference to the question of tradition. The North Americans, he maintains, constantly create and renew their national tradition. In their country tradition does not act as a brake, but rather as an accelerator and an incentive to action. On the other hand, Spanish Americans confuse tradition with stagnation.[80]

Sánchez's admiration for the United States has undoubtedly led him to overlook the fact that, in the name of tradition, influential groups in the United States have exercised considerable power in opposing significant programs of a progressive nature.

[78] Hermann Keyserling, p. 44.

[79] Luis Quintanilla, *A Latin American Speaks* (New York: Macmillan, 1943), p. 43.

[80] Luis Alberto Sánchez, *Examen espectral de América latina*, 2nd ed. (Buenos Aires: Losada, 1962), p. 157.

9

EUROPEAN AND CANADIAN VIEWS
OF THE UNITED STATES

The number of books and articles written about the United States by both natives and foreigners – diaries, impressions, commentaries – is incalculable. They go back to colonial times and extend up to the present. It can be said without exaggeration that no other people were ever so inundated by interpreters who described the habits of the inhabitants of the United States, and analyzed their character in both positive and negative terms.

At the end of the eighteenth century, the Marquis de Condorcet appealed to his countrymen to emulate the North Americans. "Oh, Frenchmen..." (he calls out) "Study the Americans of the present day...You will see to what degree of prosperity the lessons of freedom can elevate the industry of man, how they dignify his nature and dispose him to universal fraternity..."[1]

Michel Guillaume Jean de Crevecoeur, who spent half of his mature life in the United States, wrote in his *Letters from an American Farmer*, a decade before the Revolution: "What, then, is the American, this new man? He is either a European, or a descendant of a European, hence that strange mixture of blood which you will find in no other country...He is an American, who, leaving behind him all his ancient prejudices and manners, receives new ones from the new mode of life he has embraced, the new government he obeys and the new ranks he holds...Here individuals are melted into the new race of man whose labors and posterity will, one day, cause great changes in the world."[2]

The much quoted Alexis de Tocqueville was impressed by the principles of order, balance of powers, true liberty and sincere respect for justice. "I confess," he wrote in his *Democracy in America*, "that in America I saw more than America: I sought the image of democracy itself with its

---

[1] Henry Steele Commager and Elmo Giordanetti, *Was America a Mistake?* (Columbia: University of South Carolina Press, 1967), p. 40.

[2] Michel Guillaume Jean de Crevecoeur, "What is an American?", in *America in Perspective*, ed. Henry Steele Commager (New York: Random House, 1947), p. 29.

inclinations, its character, its prejudices, and its passions, in order to learn what we have to fear or to hope from its progress."[3]

Hostile comments were little more than stereotyped judgments. For example, Frances Trollope observed in her *Domestic Manners of the Americans* that although the United States was a beautiful country, its inhabitants were unbearable. America represented quantity, not quality. The men were thieves and gamblers and the women were lacking in charm. The much proclaimed democracy was a sham. One suspects that the influence of Mrs. Trollope's Tory background could not be set aside during her visit.[4]

Her son, Anthony Trollope, represented a slight improvement. "I do not like Americans...but I respect them," he wrote. In his eyes American men were crude and arrogant, and the women alert and intelligent, but crude and haughty.[5]

Mrs. Trollope's compatriot, Harriet Martineau, was on more solid ground. She pointed to the divergence between ideals and reality. "The civilization and the morals of the Americans," she asserted, "fall far below their principles." Obviously disagreeing with both Trollopes, Martineau admired the natural beauty of the American women and regretted that they were treated in a manner considerably at variance with democratic principles.[6]

Negative criticism of the United States could be traced to two sources: 1. Prejudice directed at a younger "upstart" nation, evinced by those who considered themselves culturally superior. This was often the case with European commentators; 2. Hostility and resentment in the face of the economic and military power of the United States. Frequently the feeling of cultural superiority was common to both Europeans and Spanish Americans: in the case of Europe, because that continent was historically older and richer; in the case of Spanish America, to no small degree, as a psychological defense mechanism to compensate for economic retardation and dependency.

The common complaint that the North American's passion for equality made for mediocrity was the result of a distorted view of democracy, one which produced a negative attitude toward elitist concepts and resulted in a general leveling down of talent.

It was in this connection that James Bryce, British Ambassador in Washington in the early 1900s, criticized the prominence of inferior men in U.S. politics and the absence of outstanding figures. This was due to the fact that people suffered from an optimism "which underrated the inherent difficulties

---

3   Alexis de Tocqueville, in *America in Perspective*, ed. Henry Steele Commager, p. xiii.

4   Frances Trollope, "Domestic Manners of the Americans", in Antonello Gerbi, *The Dispute of the New World: The History of a Polemic* (1759–1900). Trans. by Jeremy Moyle (Pittsburgh: The University of Pittsburgh Press, 1973), pp. 476–77.

5   Anthony Trollope, in Gerbi, pp. 488–89.

6   Harriet Martineau, in Gerbi, pp. 492–94.

of politics and failing of human nature".[7] Equality of civil rights and duties was confused with equality of capacity.

One should recognize that so-called national traits are the products of inheritance, environment and historical experience. Above all, they are culturally conditioned. On a more sophisticated level of human experience, many non-Americans seem to be in agreement in their judgment of North American character. They see the United States as the land of equality and experimentation. The country is distinguished for its hospitality and generosity. Most agree that it is the land of materialism. United States citizens have a passion for the real and the concrete; they shy away from the abstract and the ideal. "It would be better if they loved the real less and the ideal more," wrote Dickens.[8] Incidentally, Americans felt that Dickens had produced a caricature of their society, and that his notes were in bad taste. According to Henry Steele Commager, he himself regretted them subsequently.[9]

The concern for material well-being, according to many commentators, has resulted in a materialistic civilization. This oft-repeated criticism was rejected more than a century ago by the Scottish journalist Alexander Mackay, who visited the United States before the Civil War. Recording his impressions, he admits that the love of money is considered by many to be an outstanding characteristic of the American character, but then he adds: "I fear that this is a weakness to which humanity must universally plead guilty." Mackay views the United States as a country in which fortunes are yet to be made. The universal scramble to become rich is due to the belief that wealth lies within everyone's grasp. Yet, realistically, not all can become wealthy, "but all will have a chance at securing a prize".[10]

As the economic system of the United States developed, resulting in a greater degree of mechanization and standardization of life, there was a corresponding increase in the incidence of negative comments. These centered chiefly around the obsession with mass production, and a disproportionate measure of greed and arrogance, which incidentally were themselves by-products of a European capitalist system.

The popularly-held belief that the United States emphasized quantity and standardization is by no means a novel idea. However, the German scholar, Richard Müller-Freienfels, offers a more penetrating and often humorous analysis than most others.

Quantity, he maintains in his book *The Mysteries of the Soul*, written in 1927, is a *value* in the United States, not merely a fact. An object is worth

[7]   James Bryce, "The True Faults of American Democracy", in Commager, *America in Perspective*, p. 196.
[8]   Charles Dickens, in Commager, *America in Perspective*, p. xvii.
[9]   Commager, *America in Perspective*, p. 100.
[10] Alexander Mackay, "Every American is an Apostle of the Democratic Creed", in Commager, *America in Perspective*, p. 117.

more if it is large and massive. This is tied in with a concentration on the process of producing that which is practical and efficient. Technique then becomes an end in itself; the final product is standardization, the result of mass-production. Even people are standardized. "All these clean-shaven men, all these girls with their doll-like faces which are generally painted, seem to have been produced somewhere in a Ford factory, not by the dozens, but by the thousands..."[11]

At times, two commentators will offer diametrically opposed viewpoints in connection with the same trait. For example, Dickens, in speaking of the American's sense of humor, writes: "They certainly are not humorous people, and their temperament always impressed me as being of a dull and gloomy character."[12] On the other hand, James Bryce speaks in his *The American Commonwealth* of "the humorous turn of the American character. Humor is a sweetener of temper, a copious spring of charity, for it makes the good side of bad things even more visible than the weak side of good things."[13]

How do Americans react to negative judgments made about them? They are oversensitive, maintains Alexander Mackay, and travelers delight in exploiting this weakness. "The feelings of the American people have been wantonly and unnecessarily wounded by successive travelers..." Americans are not impatient of criticism, Mackay continues, provided it is fair and offered in an honest spirit. What they wince at is the application to them and their affairs of epithets tending to turn them into ridicule. Speaking of sensitivity, Mackay believes that Americans are more sensitive at home than abroad. This is balanced by the assertion that they are more boastful abroad than they are at home. "The one is a mere weakness, the other frequently, an offence."[14] Reference has already been made to the Yankee tourist, who, travelling in Europe, often exhibits an excessive amount of self-assurance. This is, perhaps, a compensatory desire to conceal an attitude of uncertainty. Europeans have a centuries-old continuity of historical experience in the face of which the North American senses his own inadequacy; he is unable to claim firm-rootedness in any older culture. "In America, there are untold millions who have not yet struck down their roots. They have not yet achieved an American form..."[15]

Criticism of the United States reached into the highest spheres, even in the realm of philosophy. Immanuel Kant joined the chorus of detractors. The American people, he affirmed, were incapable of being civilized; they were

11 Richard Müller-Freienfels, "The Mysteries of the Soul", in Commager, *America in Perspective*, p. 277.
12 Dickens, in Commager, pp. 104–05.
13 James Bryce, in Commager, p. 213.
14 Alexander Mackay, in Commager, pp. 109–10.
15 Van Wyck Brooks, in Joseph Starobin, *Paris to Peking* (New York: Cameron Associates, 1955), p. 64.

lazy and without affection and passion.[16] This was countered by Lord Byron, for whom the United States represented the last hope for freedom. Goethe, too, was so enthusiastic that he bequeathed his works to Harvard University.

Opinions of the United States and its inhabitants, as well as comparison between the two Americas, continued unabated and inundated the realm of polemics. The Spanish historian Salvador de Madariaga also jumped into the fray. An outstanding characteristic of the North American, he writes, is his mobility. The average inhabitant of the United States lives on wheels.[17] He is lacking in roots and is indifferent to tradition. He is optimistic, enthusiastic, and his belief in the inevitability of progress has assumed all the trappings of a faith. The Ibero-American, by contrast, Madariaga goes on to say, is an individual with deeply planted roots. He has brought with him his traditional values and has merged them with the Spanish American environment. He is not a nomad like his North American neighbors. Yet one must point once again to the danger involved in making snap judgments. The age of the automobile has affected Spanish-speaking populations as well. One need only cast a glance at the Paseo de la Reforma in Mexico City, or Caracas, Buenos Aires, Río de Janeiro and Santiago de Chile, to name just a few congested cities, to realize that "civilization" in the form of traffic jams and air pollution has also come to Latin America.

* * *

To complete the picture, it would be well to make reference to the attitude evinced by Canadians vis-à-vis the United States. How does the northern part of North America view its neighbors to the south? Proximity to the United States evokes similar reactions on the part of the nations on either side of the border. Both Mexico and Canada frequently reveal their uneasiness at living in the shadow of the giant. "Poor Mexico, so far from God and so close to the United States," is matched by former Canadian prime minister Pierre Elliott Trudeau's quip when he reminded a United States audience: "Living next to you is in some way like sleeping with the elephant; no matter how friendly and even-tempered the beast, one is affected by every twitch and grunt."[18]

Attitudes of Canadians with respect to their southern neighbors are ambivalent, yet they seem to reveal clearly discernable trends, resulting from changing circumstances in the political and economic areas. For example, they are directly related to a pronounced shift in the Canadian psyche toward a more pronounced nationalism, a shift which has been developing during the past several decades.

---

16 Gerbi, p. 330.
17 Salvador de Madariaga, "Presente y Porvenir de Hispanoamérica", in *Obras escogidas: Ensayos* (Buenos Aires: Editorial Sudamericana, 1972), p. 529.
18 Pierre Elliott Trudeau, *MacLean's*, July 3, 1989, p. 23.

Historically, of course, anti-U.S. attitudes had their point of origin in English Canada at the close of the American Revolution, when thousands of loyalist refugees made their way north after having been defeated. Anti-Americanism was further fomented as a source of Canadian nationhood (even under British protection) resulting from the War of 1812.

An additional factor should be borne in mind: The twentieth century witnessed the transformation of Canada from an isolationist and agricultural society to an international and economic power.[19] After World War II the discovery of oil in the province of Alberta resulted in an upsurge of foreign investment (especially by the United States), a fact which gave rise to the growth of economic nationalism, rooted in antagonism toward its southern neighbor. What the Americans have always wanted, claims a Canadian journalist, is to control Canadian resources and the profitable portions of its economy, without the trouble and expense of colonial administration.[20]

The general picture of U.S.-Canada friction contains subtle nuances, brought on by rivalries among the Canadian provinces. For example, the hostility to American investment is stronger in Ontario than in other parts of Canada, probably because Ontario is the wealthiest province in the country. On the other hand, in Quebec there is considerable support for increased investment by the United States, as a means of reducing its economic subservience to Ontario.[21]

Hugh Keenleyside, Canadian diplomat and authority on U.S.-Canadian relations, confesses that it is difficult if not impossible to render a simple explanation of a country "that can produce and give aid and avid support to both a Eugene McCarthy and a Joe McCarthy".[22] In other words, the United States, according to this observer, carries things, both good and bad, to extremes.

The term "national character" has not found much support, because its manifestations are not readily quantifiable or verifiable. Nevertheless, there seem to be certain characteristics which, by their degree of visibility and frequency of occurrence, tempt one to pause and observe, and form a very subjective impression. At the same time, one must exercise a good deal of caution and resist the tendency to draw any generalization. For example, the image which one nation has of another often borders on comfortable stereotypes which do not reflect reality. This is especially true of Canadians when they are asked to give their opinion of Americans. Stereotypes may also contradict each other. For example, Americans are seen as generous,

19 R. Scott Bornboy, "Sovereignty and Nationalism in Canada", *Current History* (March 1988), Vol. 87, p. 25.
20 Peter C. Newman, "Bold and Cautious", *MacLean's*, July 3, 1989, p. 25.
21 Payton Lyon, in *Canada-U.S. Relations*, ed., H. Edward English (New York: Praeger, 1976), p. 26.
22 *The Star-Spangled Banner*, ed. John Redekop (Toronto: Peter Martin, 1971), p. 8.

friendly, enterprising and democratic; "they are obsessed with their self-imposed burden of saving the world for democracy".[23] They are also culturally backward, lawless, obnoxious, pig-headed snobs and excessively materialistic.

Anti-U.S. feelings are noticeable in various segments of Canadian society (e.g., labor, the New Democratic Party, academic circles), because of the influence exerted by the United States in the world of trade and investment, cultural activities and military operations. A growing sense of national identity serves as a focal point of resistance to the "Americanization" of Canada. However, in matters of trade, the United States is more important to Canada than vice-versa. "American domination of foreign investment in Canada is even more pronounced than foreign trade."[24]

In the world of Canadian academia protests have been heard in the recent past and disturbing statistics offered, concerning the influx of university professors from the United States.[25] U.S. publications flood the Canadian market. Radio and television programs emanating from the States, compete with Canadian broadcasts. Ironically, many Canadians prefer the American programs. The military alliance, too, has come in for bitter criticism. The North American Air Defence Command (NORAD) is seen by some Canadians as an instrument which makes Canada dependent upon the United States, a view held by many intellectuals who are in the forefront, spearheading an awakened cultural nationalism. For them the "Americanization" of Canada means the take-over of Canadian culture by the United States. On the one hand, some Canadians are happy to have the American eagle hover over Canada protectively from a military point of view. On the other hand, others resent even its shadow. Quite a few, especially in the mass media, instrumental in the formation of public opinion, enjoy plucking the eagle's feathers, apparently Canada's favorite pastime.

And yet, despite all the resentment and hostility evinced in many quarters toward the United States, one arrives at a rather startling conclusion. Without the U.S. presence and influence, Canada might not have been so obsessed – as Margaret Atwood has put it – with taking its national pulse, with fighting for survival.[26] Ironically, too, in the same way that Canada is making efforts to maintain its own national essence in the face of the "cultural imperialism" issuing from the other side of the border, the province of Quebec is striving to assert its own national sovereignty, vis-à-vis the rest of the country.

In recent decades the populations of the United States and Canada,

[23] Newman, p. 24.

[24] J. S. Dickey and W. H. Shepardson, *Canada and the American Presence* (New York: New York University Press, 1975), p. 23.

[25] J. Steele and R. Mathews, "The Universities and the Mind", in *The Americanization of Canada*, ed. Jan Lumsden (Toronto: University of Toronto Press, 1970), pp. 170–71.

[26] Dickey and Shepardson, p. 90.

respectively, have undergone considerable change from an ethnic point of view, due to the immigration from Third World countries. Both Canadians and Americans are closer to each other than they realize. A growing number in each country favors a reduction in immigration on the grounds that racism and ethnocentricity are on the increase.[27] Canadian Human Rights commissions have warned that "racism is likely to grow as the composition of Canada's population becomes increasingly diverse".[28] As far as the United States is concerned, the frequency of racist disturbances is too well known to merit comment. In this respect, both countries have a good deal to do in the realm of developing attitude-changing techniques, designed to improve the social climate.

When all is said and done, one has to conclude that the wave of Canadian nationalism is often difficult to distinguish from anti-Americanism. In other words, is the motivation to assert one's national pride and identity positive or negative in nature? It has already been pointed out that negative origins of nationalism may lead to more positive manifestations. Even though Canadians tend to look upon the United States with a mixture of envy and superiority, one must be aware of the fact that attitudes differ between those in the East and West, between rich and poor, anglophones and francophones; nor can economic and educational factors be ignored.[29]

The negativism evinced toward the United States is also reflected in Canada's foreign policy with specific reference to the other America. In the past, Canada had declined to join the Organization of American States, partly because Canadian governments worried that membership would run the risk of putting Ottawa's foreign policy at odds with positions taken by the U.S.-dominated OAS. Until recently, the Canadian Department of External Affairs viewed the OAS as an instrument of United States foreign policy in Latin America. As a result, Canada had preferred to maintain its observer status in the organization. It did not want to be faced by the dilemma of either having to oppose the United States on particular issues, or run the risk of becoming a U.S. puppet. Yet the negative eventually developed into something positive. Canada experienced a change of heart and joined the OAS, motivated, no doubt, by a strong element of self-interest, i.e., hoping to increase its exports to Latin America.[30] Then too, Canada can, perhaps, serve as a bridge between Latin America and the United States. It is ideally suited to perform the role of mediator in any sort of discordant situation which may develop between the two Americas.

---

27 Hilary MacKenzie, "The Racist Underside", *MacLean's*, June 25, 1990, p. 80.
28 MacKenzie, p. 83.
29 Rea Corelli, "A Border of Mirrors", *MacLean's*, Jan. 1, 1990, pp. 37–38.
30 Ross Laver, "A Seat at the Table", *MacLean's*, Oct. 16, 1989, p. 24.

10

THE TWO AMERICAS:
OLD HABITS, NEW CHALLENGES

In order to perpetuate a harmonious relationship between the two Americas, it is first necessary to put an end to the economic underdevelopment of Spanish America, a historical fact which also has its cultural and psychological repercussions. The United States shares the responsibility for this condition. It has frequently looked with disdain upon Spanish America. It has sent troops to "defend its interests", determined the political orientation of governments, and promoted policies which provoked hostility on the part of progressive sectors of the continent. Conversely, many Spanish Americans have been guilty of adding fuel to the fires of antagonism out of sheer ignorance, i.e., accepting facile explanations concerning the nature of United States society which border on the caricature, rather than analyzing the complex structure of the country to the North.

The "romantic temperament" of Spanish Americans has too often substituted the "sound of fury" of bombastic rhetoric for discussion and persuasion. A love-hate relationship can be said to characterize the Spanish American attitude toward its northern neighbor. On the one hand, the latter represents the land of opportunity for those who succeed in entering the country. On the other hand, the Spanish American believes that Yankee wealth is the cause of poverty and suffering of his own people. He is likewise convinced of his cultural superiority which, in his eyes, is more valuable than the material wealth of the United States. This comfortable subterfuge acts to immobilize him and frees him of all responsibility to attempt to eradicate the social ills which continue to victimize the land.[1]

The emphasis on material success to the neglect and detriment of ethical values is not a monopoly of the United States. It pervades other portions of the globe as well. It is not very popular to point to the fact that the Spanish American Calibans cooperate with those of the United States, Great Britain,

---

[1] Mario Vargas Llosa, "La amistad difícil", *Ideas*, University of Miami, 2, No. 1 (1988), pp. 2–3.

Germany, Japan and others. It has long been convenient to place the blame for all of Spanish America's ills on the United States.

The average North American, too, is a captive of distorted imagery and stereotyped thinking vis-à-vis the Spanish American, which act as barriers to mutual understanding and respect. Terrorists, drug dealers and bikini-clad beauties contribute to the composite picture which shapes the myth and the prejudice.

Spanish America must realize that if it is to choose democracy as a way of life, as opposed to totalitarianism, it must effect a close degree of cooperation with open and democratic societies, including the United States. Conversely, the United States must realize that cooperation and solidarity are not the equivalent of servitude. Spanish America is not a satellite.

* * *

At one point capitalist development might have been considered a progressive force, resulting in social and economic improvements. However, it has, with the passage of time, acquired negative characteristics, which have been over-developed, ushering in as a result a period of dehumanization; technology now controls man. It is therefore incumbent upon Americans, both North and South, to resist this type of capitalist expansion. Unfortunately, the American of the North who is aware of this development is still in the minority. He needs help to resist chaos and demoralization, and enlightened Spanish Americans must be prepared to give it to him. In both Americas this struggle will be the work of minorities, since it has always been the task of enlightened minorities to be aware of the need for reform. Working together represents the hope for both Americas. In a spirit of mutual respect they can, perhaps, put America back on track in the sense of granting moral and esthetic values their rightful place. Only when the individual will no longer be viewed exclusively as a means to an end, but as an end in himself, will the American ideal be realized.

The popular belief that the United States represents the spirit of utilitarianism and technology, which finds its highest expression in Rodó's *Ariel*, continues to persist, despite attempts to show that there are also humanistic values to be found in the "Colossus of the North".

It has therefore been relatively easy for some Spanish Americans to choose between capitalist imperialism and the socialist ideal. However, as recent events have shown, the choice has become more complicated. Socialist systems have undergone many gyrations and have revealed glaring violations of human rights. One Bolivian essayist has stated that in the Old World socialism is equal to slavery and despotism. However, he consoles himself in the belief that in the New World it represents liberation and social justice, and that a new humanism is being born, combined with a nationalism situated somewhere between capitalist imperialism and the Soviet formula.[2]

Regardless of differences in political philosophy or ethnic composition, the republics of Spanish America have this much in common, and to this extent it can be said that they share a cultural identity: they are all seeking ways – and if they are not, they should – to determine and control their own social and economic destiny, to eliminate, or at least diminish, domination by foreign capital, to achieve some measure of agrarian reform, to improve education and public health, and finally, rid themselves of political corruption and military rule.

How will all this be accomplished? The solutions attempted will not be the same for all. Each nation will select its own path and elaborate its program in accordance with its own set of circumstances and in a moment of history which it deems convenient and opportune.

The Spanish American republics are not underdeveloped, and yet they are not entirely free of certain aspects characteristic of underdeveloped countries. What is striking – and this is not peculiar to Spanish America alone – is the uneasy mixture of technical and industrial development of some countries, coupled with the social backwardness and economic stagnation peculiar to various regions of the continent. Whether or not the transformation of political and economic structures will be effected through peaceful means or otherwise will depend on the distribution and development of social forces within each country, as well as the economic interests of foreign powers which attempt to influence the course of events within these countries.

* * *

Pan Americanism which was meant to foster inter-American cooperation had its point of origin in the United States. Supposedly a descendant of the Monroe Doctrine, it was looked upon with suspicion by the southern half of the hemisphere. If, at first, Spanish Americans accepted on faith the purported reason for the Monroe Doctrine, namely, the exclusion of foreign, i.e., European, penetration into Latin America, the U.S.-Mexican War, as well as the various cases of U.S. intervention, convinced them that penetration was reserved for the powerful nation to the north.

Pan Americanism eventually metamorphosed into the Organization of American States. Yet any interaction between the two Americas seemed to operate only in one direction – from North to South – economically and politically. Some Spanish Americans, especially those who wished to resist this current and thereby assert their national identity, argue that a united federated Spanish America would act as a brake against U.S. domination.

---

2 Fernando Díez de Medina, "Europa y América, dos polos culturales", in *El ensayo actual latinoamericano*, ed. Ernesto Mejía Sánchez (México: Andrea, 1971), p. 41.

They maintain that the United States prefers a disunited continent in the economic sense, since it is more advantageous to keep Spanish America divided. It is financially more profitable for the United States to deal with Spanish American nations individually, since in the absence of a federated union, they are more vulnerable. On the other hand, if they were to be united in one federation, thus echoing the dream of Bolívar, they would be in a position to resist more effectively the attempts by their northern neighbor to exploit the continent. In short, federation is an effective way in which Spanish America could rid itself of the inferior role it plays vis-à-vis the North.[3] Of course, it must be remembered that there are always powerful elements that prefer to deal with the United States unilaterally, because of the advantages which *they* would receive. Their action would constitute a detriment to the hoped-for integration of the continent, and an obstacle to the friendship and cooperation on a mutual basis between the two Americas.

The foreign policy of the United States can be said to have been characterized by a series of zig-zags in the course of the past two centuries. U.S. attitudes, like those of any other nation, were determined, not by subjective traits located in the personality make-up of its citizens, but rather by the political and economic interests of the nation. The trajectory of United States-Spanish American relations reveals ups and downs, the result of domestic and foreign circumstances. Friendly interest in the movement for Spanish American independence was followed by patronizing attitudes which considered Spanish America as the backyard of the United States. North American overt expansionist policies alternated with a more subtle Pan Americanism. William James's characterization concerning the "tough-minded" and the "tender-minded" had their counterparts in leading political circles which formulated United States foreign policy.

Relations between the two Americas must be viewed against the background of international tensions prevailing at the close of the twentieth century. The second half of the present century has been characterized by the competing claims for the allegiance and loyalty of the world's population advanced by rival ideologies and socio-political systems. Of course, these antagonists and their allies and supporters do not constitute a homogeneous force. There are divergences and tensions within each camp, testifying to the fluidity and fluctuations characteristic of the world of politics. History is witness to the fact that since nothing is permanent in this area, the dominant nations of today will not necessarily be the same tomorrow. Babylonia, Greece and Egypt, to cite but a few examples from the ancient world, and Spain, France and England, in modern times, illustrate this phenomenon – a fact from which many Spanish Americans may derive some comfort. The latter believe that if only their respective nations could somehow forge some

3   Eduardo Caballero Calderón, "Latinoamérica, un mundo por hacer", in *Obras* (Medellín: Editorial Bebout, 1963), pp. 40–41.

degree of political and economic unity, they too could achieve a measure of greatness, denied them at present. However, they are sufficiently realistic to realize that this is no more than a quixotic dream as far as the immediate future is concerned.

It is at this point that the United States enters the picture. Spanish American thinkers are aware that in very real terms it is the "Colossus of the North" that guides the destinies of the republics to the South. Economic and political pressures, as well as military intervention, are calculated to insure that Spanish American countries remain in the North American sphere of influence. From the vantage point of the United States, this is a logical position to adopt – one which serves to protect its national interests.

However, there is another side to the coin, one which is perhaps utopian, but nevertheless entertained hopefully by not a few Spanish Americans. Spanish America could conceivably help the United States more effectively – and itself as well – if it were economically and politically more independent, and if it were permitted to evolve into a continental community. It would then be more than a mere supplier of raw materials, exploited for the benefit of the industrial north. This would imply a giant step forward in the direction of liquidating the superior mentality complex manifested toward "colonial" peoples.[4]

A possible solution in the direction of remedial action would be the establishment of regional bodies which would deal with economic problems, housing resources, public health and cultural exchange. This would be a first step in stimulating a collective awareness of the need to put an end to the subordinate position in which Spanish America finds itself.

Another course of action has been suggested by those economists who favor an increased degree of privatization and a diminished measure of control by the state apparatus. The State in Latin America has always enacted laws that favor special interest groups, rather than the general public. This practice is labelled "mercantilism" by Hernando de Soto, a leading authority on the problem of dependency in Latin America (See below Appendix E). "Mercantilism" is characterized by a bureaucratized state that regards the redistribution of wealth as more important than the production of wealth. It "condemns a society to economic stagnation and imposes relations between citizens and the State that reduce the possibility of democratic politics".[5] The alternative program, advocated by de Soto, would involve the establishment of a system which "transfers to private individuals those

---

4   It remains to be seen how NAFTA (North American Free Trade Agreement) will affect hemispheric relations.

5   Mario Vargas Llosa, "Forward", in Hernando de Soto, *The Other Path* (New York: Harper & Row, 1989), p. xv.

responsibilities and initiatives which the state has thus far monopolized unsuccessfully."[6]

* * *

The question of U.S. intervention in Spanish America has a long and not so venerable history. The many instances in which the United States has intervened either directly or indirectly offer more than ample substantiation of a policy adopted by a super power, acting in accord with its interests. Mexico, Cuba, the Dominican Republic, Grenada, Nicaragua, El Salvador, Guatemala and Panama are but several examples which have served to increase resentment and harden negative attitudes in significant sectors of Spanish America – so much so that "U.S. bashing" has become a tradition.

Despite the fact that it may be argued that the use of military force was unjustified in these cases, a counter-argument may be advanced, namely, that intervention as a principle, should not be considered in absolute terms, i.e., that it is always bad and undesirable. Introducing a relativist approach in the evaluation of the principle of intervention carries with it certain risks. One would have to weigh the circumstances surrounding each case of intervention; each judgment would be bound to result in controversy. Yet viewing intervention in absolute terms, i.e., as a policy to be opposed under all circumstances, seems equally invalid. Not to intervene, at times, may yield even more tragic results than open intervention in the affairs of a foreign country. England and France signed a non-intervention agreement at the outbreak of the Spanish Civil War when the Republican government desperately needed military assistance. Germany and Italy did intervene and the results of the "dress rehearsal" for World War II were a foregone conclusion.

When we boycott South African products or withdraw our investments from that country as a protest against "Apartheid", we are intervening. When the Soviet Union intervened in Afghanistan, the United States reportedly furnished military aid to the Afghan rebels. The United States helped the "contras" in Nicaragua; the Cubans were said to have aided the Sandinistas – all of these, obvious cases of intervention. One might well ask at this point: If the United States were to oppose a Latin American military dictator (regardless of its motives) and would attempt to overthrow him, would the rest of Latin America still cry "intervention"? Is intervention by a *Latin American* country in the affairs of a neighbor justified if such action is designed to rid the area of a military dictator? The question is, indeed, a thorny one and worthy of discussion. (See Appendix D).

* * *

6   Hernando de Soto, pp. 245–46.

For many decades the concept of socialism projected an image of a righteous world devoid of injustice, a concept for which countless generations were willing to sacrifice themselves. It acquired a mystique and all the trappings of a religion: it had its prophets, charismatic leaders, heretics and traitors. Its faith was bolstered by an invincible belief that history was on its side.

For some firm believers, the events of 1989 merely represented a temporary setback in the inexorable march from capitalism to socialism. Mismanagement by government functionaries did not invalidate the theory. For many others the trauma must have been unbearable. Socialist regimes turned out to be corrupt systems, run by cynical, opportunistic bureaucrats who appropriated all the material comforts, while the rest of the population lived in economic misery. The one-party system violated human rights with the aid of the military and the dreaded secret police. This was a betrayal of socialism according to some who still cling to their lifelong ideal. But the bubble had burst. The people rebelled against the Communist State; reform-minded Communists fought against bureaucratic Communists, and nationalists fought against both.

Yet throughout the duration of this debacle, one is struck by the fact that the United States, that representative par excellence of capitalism and free enterprise, did not rejoice (at least publicly) at the failure of its ideological enemy. It did not rub its hands in glee at the collapse of the Communist regimes. On the contrary, it sent goods and funds to the countries affected, to assist in their economic recovery. Of course, one may question whether the motives were purely altruistic. One wonders, however, whether the Communist world would have been so generous with its financial assistance if the situation had been reversed, i.e., if the capitalist world were to find itself on the verge of economic catastrophe. Does not Marxist-Leninist dogma speak of the inevitable demise of capitalism? We will overtake and surpass the United States, Soviet theoreticians had proclaimed in the past. "We will bury you," Nikita Khrushchev had exclaimed, exultantly. Yet the United States, regardless of its motives, welcomed the advance of democratic currents in Eastern Europe. This runs counter to the charge, often advanced in Latin America, namely, that the United States has always been and continues to be interested in freedom and democracy, but only for itself.

With these European developments as a background, it may now be more feasible to take a second look at the United States-Spanish America equation. Since the end of World War II, the United States (and the west in general) had based its foreign policy upon the hypothesis that the Soviets might invade western Europe. The Communist threat had to be contained in Latin America as well. Now that the U.S.S.R. has collapsed, it would seem unlikely for the remnants to embark upon policies calculated to encourage Communist movements in Latin America. In these circumstances the Communist "menace" in Latin America which has so obsessed the United States, may indeed be exaggerated. It should be borne in mind that radical movements in Latin America may be "home-grown". They do not need encouragement from Moscow. Perhaps the United States can now encourage the growth of social democratic movements in Latin America, instead of throwing its support behind extreme right-wing political movements.

The astounding collapse of the Communist regimes is bound to affect the leftist movement in Latin America. The crisis suffered by the Communist governments of East Germany, Hungary, Poland, Albania, Yugoslavia and Czechoslovakia, the political uncertainty which characterizes the governments of Roumania and Bulgaria, and finally the Pandora's box which Mikhail Gorbachev opened in the U.S.S.R. itself and which led to its downfall, have understandably left the Latin American Communist Parties in a confused situation. Castro's Cuba seems more isolated than ever and determined to "go it alone". The Sandinista government has been replaced by a victorious opposition, the government of El Salvador has made peace with the rebels. In short, the continent has witnessed an upsurge in democratic, reform-minded sentiment, and a consequent weakening or elimination of military dictatorship as, for example, in the cases of Argentina, Chile and Brazil. However, as of this writing, constitutional government has been suspended in Peru.

If the Spanish American Communist movement per se appears to have lost some of its effectiveness, partially perhaps because of events in Europe, then it becomes incumbent upon the United States to modify its policy vis-à-vis the leftist movements generally. If Ronald Reagan's reference to the Soviet Union as the "evil empire" has given way to a halt in the Cold War, then certainly the time has come for the United States to alter its image radically insofar as Spanish America is concerned.

This seems to be a propitious moment for Washington to take a daring step forward to convince the progressive elements of Latin America that it, too, is interested in advancing the cause of social and economic betterment for the people of that continent, that it no longer labels any effort at improvement as "Communist inspired", and that it will not lend its support to extreme right-wing movements or governments in their battle against "subversive" elements.

There is a vast body of liberal-leftist thought in Spanish America which would welcome enthusiastically any moral and political sympathy emanating from the United States. The democratic ideals, long associated with the United States, and considered by many Spanish Americans to have been abandoned and betrayed, can now be revived.

This is an excellent opportunity for the long festering anti-United States hostility to be assuaged and replaced by a more positive attitude. It is high time for the United States to stop seeing a Communist conspiracy in every attempt to implement land reform, social legislation, civil liberties or even economic measures which smack of socialistic tendencies.

The Mexican writer, Carlos Fuentes, has put it very succinctly. The United States, he feels, has been remiss in recognizing the need for change, and that the bearer of this change in its cultural context is nationalism. Such a perspective calls for a flexible policy of diplomatic negotiations to resolve points of conflict. The result would be a strengthening of independent states, each building its institutions of stability and renewing its culture of national identity. The United States has, likewise, failed to identify the problems of international redistribution of power as these affect Latin America. Are right-wing governments, he asks in this connection, the sole legitimate representative of Latin American nationalism? Are they the only friends that can be claimed by the powerful nation to the north? Speaking at a Harvard University commencement in 1983, Fuentes declared: "The United States has true friends in this hemisphere. Friends, not satellites."[7]

It is time to resist the temptation to indulge in snap judgments and stereotyped thinking. These can lead to ludicrous conclusions and amusing distortions of logic. In the case of the two Americas, the following set of syllogisms will serve to illustrate how emotional attitudes and ideological conditioning, characterized by distrust and suspicion, can result in faulty reasoning. The United States, with reference to Latin America, thinks that:

> Nationalism equals anti-Americanism
> Anti-Americanism equals Communism
> Therefore: Nationalism equals Communism.

Spanish Americans are equally guilty in believing that

> Anti-Communism equals pro-Americanism
> Pro-Americanism equals Imperialism
> Therefore: Anti-Communism equals Imperialism.[8]

There is a strong likelihood that if the United States renders assistance to Eastern Europe as well as to the Persian Gulf area, Spanish America may find itself at a financial disadvantage. This possibility becomes painfully evident in view of the huge national deficit incurred by the United States. An interruption in the granting of economic aid to Spanish America may well result in an increase of anti-democratic sentiment. For this reason, the United States should not hesitate to help not only "privatized" enterprises and free market economies, but also state subsidized ventures.

Where the private sector is still relatively ineffectual because it operates in a so-called underdeveloped country, it may be necessary for the state to supervise and control the economic activities of the nation. Such a system of

7   Carlos Fuentes, *Myself With Other*, *Selected Essays* (New York: The Noonday Press, Farrar, Strauss and Giroux, 1990), p. 213.
8   Victor Alba, *Nationalists Without Nations* (New York: Praeger, 1968), pp. 16–17.

"state capitalism" may be progressive in character, as opposed to monopoly capitalism, managed by powerful financial corporations.

In any case, the point is that the United States foreign policy should be more flexible, allowing for a variety of approaches, one of which would include cooperation with liberal-left governments. If U.S. President Bush could cooperate with Russian president Yeltsin, then the United States should be able to get along with even a moderate socialist regime in Spanish America, if one should materialize.

* * *

It has long been a truism to state that in both the capitalist and socialist camps talk is often at variance with deeds. For example, in the capitalist orbit people speak of liberalism in spite of glaring examples to the contrary which are to be found in that system. In the so-called socialist societies lip service is paid to the loftiest humanitarian ideals – a supremely ironic commentary in view of what has happened in Eastern Europe and in the former Soviet Union. In the Third World discontent is still prevalent. Within each of these worlds there is a conflict between the dominant groups that are interested primarily in preserving their positions of power and those which adopt a more enlightened posture. The centuries-old drama continues to be played out: orthodoxy, fundamentalism and traditionalism versus dissidence, reform and heresy.

In this context, the concept of nationalism acquires a potency to be exploited by the various competing socio-political groups. Both radical and conservative forces claim that they are the true heirs of the national tradition. National values become an instrument to be utilized for the purpose of improving or advancing the cause of social betterment. Thus, an authentic national awareness can be developed in conjunction with positive policies involving the welfare of the great mass of people, or it can be distorted by the cultivation of a pseudo-patriotism in the interests of a particular group in society.

In this connection, the old political terms "left" and "right" seem to have lost their meaning. Their use serves to nurture a sentimental attachment to idealistic ideologies. In the eyes of the adherents of socialist thought, "leftism" has always been associated with progress and reform; those of the "right" were always considered conservative, if not reactionary and "anti-people". In recent decades, however, this distinction has been blurred. For example, political regimes of "rightist" inspiration have continued in power with populist support. "Socialist" regimes have been guilty of the most scandalous behavior in the treatment of their citizens. "Dissidents" have been condemned as "counter-revolutionary", executed and subsequently "rehabilitated", as a result of a change in the dominant "party line". It has long been obvious that it is not enough to want to change the system in order to effect progress of any kind. In recent decades it has become painfully clear that it is necessary to change the people who want to change the system.

For five centuries Spanish Americans have been spectators. With the dawn of the twenty-first century in sight it is hoped that they will take their rightful place as actors on the stage of history.

However, in order to realize this, it will be necessary for ordinary Spanish Americans to recognize the demagogue when he appears upon the scene, to discriminate between democratically-minded leaders and corrupt politicians, and not be swayed by excesses of rhetoric. They will have to learn to be sufficiently sophisticated not to allow anti-imperialist slogans to drive a wedge between themselves and the people of the United States. They will have to be astute enough not to permit themselves to fall into linguistic traps, such as is the case, e.g., when a dictator speaks of "direct democracy", or when torture of political prisoners is referred to as "interrogation".

* * *

A sober examination of the entire complex configuration involved in national or cultural awareness and identity will inevitably lead to the conclusion that it is more than a common language that holds people together. It has been pointed out on innumerable occasions that there is usually no one language or culture that is common to all. In Paraguay, for example, the people speak Guaraní as well as Spanish. In certain other areas, Aymará, Quiché and Quechua are spoken.

In Latin America the language which binds people together transcends Latin derivatives or indigenous tongues. A military dictator and an inhabitant of a "villa miseria" may both speak Spanish, but they do not have much else in common. The true language which acts as a unifying force is the language of democracy, the language of freedom and justice, a language which has yet to be realized.

One can speak of partial or relative realization of this ideal, or realization in stages, more advanced in some countries than in others. However, the ideal continues to be a stimulus and a goal in both Americas. The struggle to achieve power in order to implement the ideals of liberty, justice and peace is, in the last analysis, the essence of America.

Any attempt to define Spanish American cultural identity in ethnic terms is bound to result in an exercise leading to frustration. For example, some essayists have spoken of a "cosmic culture",[9] applying Vasconcelos's concept of a "cosmic race" to the socio-political realm. This type of syncretism which mixes different sects and religions, and endeavors to assimilate racial

9 For example, Orlando Fallas Borda, "Sentido actual de la identidad cultural", *Cuadernos Americanos*, México, 239, No. 6 (1981), pp. 18–22.

types and culture patterns, overlooks the strong possibility that some of the elements to be "mixed" may be incompatible.

Judging the problem of cultural identity from a purely ethnic perspective seems inadequate and far from satisfactory. One may well ask at this point: is there any social system which, more than any other, favors and cultivates a wholesome cultural identity? The answer seems obvious. If, for example, the modern media are in the hands of foreign interests, if foreign commercial and industrial powers continue to exert pressures upon Spanish American society, then the development of the cultural identity of its inhabitants is impeded; in fact, it can be arrested to the extent that it allows itself to be led in undesirable directions. In short, foreign influences and pressures can result in traumatic experiences for the Spanish American who is striving to realize his national awareness to the full and to take his rightful place in the cultural sun.

When one attempts to draw up a balance sheet with respect to such concepts as "identity" and "essence", one comes away with the feeling that any attempt to postulate a national character turns out to be a questionable exercise. There are too many variables: racial, ethnic and religious. There are differences in geographic sections and social classes. For example, those who would examine Spanish American reality from only one point of view or in terms of only one historical tradition, are guilty of the grossest of errors. The racial elements of this continent have combined in varying degrees to form new racial types. The number of ethnic variations and combinations is fascinating, both mathematically and esthetically.

In spite of the differences which separate North Americans from Spanish Americans, one cannot deny that there are certain ideals and aspirations which unite them: dignity, social justice, freedom. Of course, democracy is not yet a reality in the Western Hemisphere. There are still battles to be fought before true liberty can be said to exist in every part of the continent. Nevertheless, these ideals have been realized imperfectly and incompletely. It is for this reason that America as a whole has come to symbolize these ideals. This is its true mission: the hope that they may be attained to an optimum degree by everyone concerned.

The problem of cultural identity is thus related to the struggle by the Spanish American republics to forge their own destiny. This involves the elimination, or, at least, diminution of corruption and military rule, transformation of the landowning system by means of agrarian reform, improvement of educational and public health standards, and promotion of the industrialization of the continent. Such industrialization would have to imply the development of domestic markets, possibly within various regional groupings, since existing markets outside the continent are controlled by foreign interests.

If Spanish America is to exercise any sort of creative role in effective fashion, it would seem that it would do so best by means of opposing the expansionist interests of its northern neighbor. This would constitute one

more step in the process of moulding Spanish American identity, one conceived in terms of freedom to develop, instead of acquiring and accepting
the role of a colonial appendage.[10]

For decades Spanish America found itself in a position of dependency. Its
role, imposed by the economically more developed nations, has been that of
providing raw materials for exports and importing manufactured goods. The
cultural sequel has been a lack of democratization in the life of the continent,
characterized by chronic political instability. To the political factor must be
added the socio-economic variable in the form of internal oligarchies that are
quite willing to cooperate with powerful corporations abroad, thus placing
their class interests above national welfare. They are content to see their respective nations cast in the role of passive objects rather than active subjects.

Political and economic emancipation go hand-in-hand with efforts to
define and defend the cultural identity of Spanish America. National interre-
lationships, as countermeasures to continental fragmentation, can serve to
further crystallize and strengthen this identity. In the process, each republic
should be free to choose the social system which best insures the preservation of its culture. Necessary mechanisms will be created by governments as
well as by cultural institutions, which will strive to implement programs
toward that end.

Economic rivalries and conflicts have their repercussions in the realm of
political action, as well as in the area of ideological fermentation. In the case
of the latter, leading Spanish American intellectuals have wanted to integrate
their continent into the mainstream of Europe's history of ideas. However, as
has been indicated, there are also those of a more nationalistic persuasion
who have attempted to formulate and create an "American" system of
thought, i.e., an "original" and "authentic" continental philosophy. A third
group has endeavored to reconcile these two polarities and synthesize the
best elements of both orientations.

The Spanish American had the notion that he was a creature without a
history, tradition or past. In many cases he was persuaded to look at himself
through European eyes. The Mexican, for example, suffered from a sense of
inferiority because he saw in America only what Europe wished to see, and
Europe saw only a Utopia, not a reality. This reality was something inferior
and of little value. For this reason he sought to imitate foreign models in the
belief that these were superior to his own reality.[11]

Europeanization of Spanish America was the dream of those who would
usher in a period of progress and prosperity. Such Europeanization was
identified with the spirit of modernity, the rise of the bourgeoisie, and the

[10] Abelardo Villegas, *Autognosis: el pensamiento mexicano en el siglo XX* (México: Instituto Panamericano de Geografía e Historia, 1985), p. 126.

[11] Abelardo Villegas, *La filosofía de lo mexicano* (México: Fondo de Cultura Económica,
1960), p. 157.

development of capitalism, science and democracy; in short, Spanish American thinkers attributed a universal quality to Western culture which they sought to imitate.

The end of the Cold War and the collapse of the Communist governments in Europe could not have failed to leave an impression on Hispanic America. Furthermore, the capitalist West has had its own political and economic complications. For example, the European Common Market is seeking to shore up its structure. The United States is attempting to regroup its interests by fostering the adoption of a Trade Pact involving Mexico and Canada. These developments are not lost upon Latin America as a whole which still asks itself how much longer it will be considered as an object of booty.

* * *

As the twentieth century enters its last decade, the United States must take stock of itself as a world power and of its role in history in the context of the dynamic changes which are taking place. It must be ready to adjust to new circumstances on the international arena and, if necessary, learn new habits and acquire new attitudes. This will come about as events leave their impact; it will help if the nation engages in self-analysis, and if its citizens take to heart some of the commentaries offered by foreign critics, as well as by their own compatriots.

Such modification of behavior is necessary, especially if North America is to understand the problems of Latin America. It may also be a painful process, since the cost of adaptation is high. Understanding must be reciprocal, and it must lead to action if it is to be effective. Understanding is not enough in itself, "but it is an indispensable beginning".[12] What is important is the future of the continent, not the past or even the present. It is essential to bid farewell to narrow-minded nationalism or outworn traditions. What matters is an on-going dynamic evolving process, the forging of a new type of human being – and this for the North as well as for the South. North America will have to move over and allow Latin America to share the stage. Only then will the Old World realize that the New World, America, is not merely a static geographic entity, but a historical, developmental process, a moment in the direction of realizing much-needed humane values.

As pointed out elsewhere in this essay, the attempts to strengthen humanistic values have always been the task of a creative minority, regardless of which of the two Americas is under consideration. The emphasis on materialistic drives must be resisted lest these threaten to overwhelm us and convert the human being into an inanimate object, a cog in a gigantic machine. The creative minority, therefore, needs help in order to make its influence felt to a greater extent. If this seems to be especially urgent in the United

12   D. W. Brogan, *The American Character* (New York: Knopf, 1950), p. 169.

States, it is no less applicable to the Spanish American scene. The creative minorities of *both* Americas need each other in order to build more effectively the necessary dykes which will contain the flood waters of materialism and technology.

The distribution of forces is too lop-sided. The equilibrium must be restored. We have become slaves to the computer. The more sensitive elements of the two Americas must share with each other their dreams and perceptions of beauty, truth and human dignity, although it would seem that it is incumbent upon the North American sector to show more initiative in this respect. It is the North that is more aggressive and influential in the realm of the materialistic and exploitative.

Progressive sectors in the United States must do everything in their power to counteract the somewhat ironic accusation, advanced in many quarters, that the democratic principles of the United States seem to have become mummified, precisely at the moment when these very principles have inspired submerged peoples to become democratic republics, opposed to United States imperialism. It is sad to see the British historian Arnold Toynbee give voice to the belief that the United States has betrayed its revolution and its democratizing mission. "The United States is today the head of an anti-revolutionary movement, operating in defense of selfish interests..."[13]

It is indeed a pity that the United States has failed to recognize that the principles embodied in the Declaration of Independence are not theirs alone; that the Declaration should be offered generously to all peoples, regardless of which portion of the globe they inhabit. Perhaps if these democratic principles were proclaimed to all sectors of the world's population, irrespective of political, economic or racial configuration, the image of the North American would be less of a caricature and more of a portrait of what he really is.

From the Spanish American perspective, the Jekyll-Hyde syndrome is a cruel trick played upon the United States by history, namely presenting a dual image of that country as the cradle of liberty as opposed to a rapacious nation embarked upon imperialist policies and plagued by the curse of racism.

It is time for both Americas to engage in a re-examination of their real or fancied psychological complexes. It would be best if the Spanish Americans gave up their supposed economic and political inferiority complex, and for the United States to lose its alleged cultural inferiority complex. This process seems to have begun in various degrees. What is needed is additional motivation and momentum in order that these distinct societies learn from one another, and thus advance their relationship in a positive manner. It remains to be seen what gains, if any, will be achieved as a result of the crises

---

13   Quoted in Ribero, *The Americas and Civilization* (New York: Dutton, 1971), pp. 387–88.

suffered by the various Communist regimes in Europe, and the repercussions felt in the Americas.

At a moment in contemporary history when human yearning for a greater measure of freedom and democracy is on the march in what was formerly the Communist world, Latin America still seems unable to prevent growing social and economic deterioration within its borders. Without economic development, prospects for Latin American democracy remain grim. True, military dictatorships in the past few years have yielded to democratic forms of government. Unfortunately, the countries involved have also suffered increasing impoverishment, so that democracy has become more identified with poverty than with liberty.

Added to the general picture of economic hardship and social strife are the expansion of the illicit trade in drugs and the increase of terrorist activities. The growing radicalization of the poor, the potentially fertile ground for the breeding of populist demagogues, and the possible resurgence of the military, all combine to convert the continent into an ominous powder keg.[14]

Can the two Americas work together to prevent social and economic upheaval in Latin America? The United States may conceivably contribute to a solution, at least partially so, by reducing payments on Latin American debts. However, Latin America must be willing and ready to undertake economic reforms. For example, adjustments must be made to curb bloated bureaucracies. The income tax system must be overhauled and tax returns controlled more efficiently. Funds urgently needed to inject into the economic system should not be allowed to leave the continent and be deposited in Swiss banks.

In spite of the apparently gloomy picture of the United States painted by some of the ideological enemies of that country, peoples of the world still associate it with personal freedom and democratic government. These ideas are still in the ascendency, even though the United States economy may be shaky, its social fabric challenged periodically by racial conflicts, and it may not be the superpower it once was.

In short, what is called for is a New World in every sense of the term, a world free from racial and political prejudice, from narrow-minded national-ism, and divisiveness and disintegration. Although pettiness and magna-nimity will exist as long as humans populate the earth, and will continue to battle for the possession of man's soul, efforts must constantly be made to alter the equation. Responsibility and consideration for the "other" must gain in importance as opposed to egotism and decadence. The see-saw battle which goes on in society, on both an individual and collective scale, will have to be resolved in positive fashion if the New World is not to be a facsimile of the "Old".

---

14 See George de Lama, "Latin World on the Edge of an Abyss", *Chicago Tribune*, June 4, 1989, p. 27.

APPENDIX A:
CONCERNING THE "FRONTIER THESIS" OF
FREDERICK JACKSON TURNER

The image of the American as an individualist may be traced directly to the influence of an agrarian philosophy prevailing at the time of Thomas Jefferson. The abundance of land and resources tended to encourage the development of the individual personality, pitted against the forces of the wilderness. The individualism and idealism of Jeffersonian democracy were reflected in such folklore heroes as Daniel Boone and Davy Crockett.

The picture of the pioneer – freedom-loving, self-reliant and egalitarian – was reinforced by the frontier thesis of Frederick Jackson Turner, which appeared in 1893. The thesis stressed the nineteenth-century Westward Movement into the primitive areas as being the most important element.[1] The frontiersman, rugged and self-sufficient, played an essential role in promoting democracy. An individualist, he naturally was opposed to authority if he felt that this interfered with his activities.

The spirit of individualism was closely allied with that of egalitarianism, another facet of American identity which, Turner claimed, was promoted by the Westward Movement. Egalitarianism, as a basic tenet of the American Creed, is based on the belief that all men are alike in the eyes of the Creator. Ingrained in the Creed is the denial that some individuals are better than others. Everyone is possessed of a certain dignity, no matter what his or her circumstances may be.

This would explain the rejection of authority and the notion that some are born to command and others merely to serve. For example, the dislike of the officer class in the military is an expression of the American belief in equality.[2] In a way, resistance to authority is nothing new in American life. It was an attitude manifested by the framers of the Constitution. The British sociologist Geoffrey Gorer, after having visited the United States, came away with the impression that Americans are allergic to authority. "...Authority is inherently bad and dangerous; the survival and growth of the state

---

1 Frederick Jackson Turner, *The Significance of the Frontier in American History* (New York: Frederick Ungar, 1963), p. 3.

2 David M. Potter, "The Quest for the National Character", in John Higham, *The Reconstruction of American History* (London: Hutchinson, 1963), pp. 215–16.

133

make it inevitable that some individuals must be endowed with authority; but this authority must be...limited...and the holders of these positions... should be watched as potential enemies."[3]

Turner's thesis, attractive though it may be, has been criticized by eminent American scholars. These have charged that the argument advanced seems too simple because of its emphasis on geographical determinism. The frontiersman was overly romanticized and idealized. Accentuating the geographic and climatic factors, and ignoring the European background and influence, did not tell the whole story as far as the formation of the American character was concerned.

Turner's defenders rallied to stem the criticism. Once the forests were cleared and the West conquered, they maintained, the rough Frontiersman would have more time to develop cultural refinement. Yet this line of reasoning allows for an uncomfortable implication: the emphasis on the priority of material well being rarely leaves room for the development of the finer values, thereby giving additional weight to the belief that the American is primarily a crude materialist. To put it mercilessly, the Turner thesis would suggest that the pioneer and the settler were most American when they were least cultivated.[4]

As for the claim that the advance of the frontier promoted democracy,[5] it has been affirmed that, on the contrary, democracy did not come out of the forest; it was carried there. "On some frontiers democracy was not strengthened...Free land gave the opportunity to establish slavery in Louisiana, oligarchy in the Mormon state, the hacienda system in Mexican California...."[6]

Admittedly, westward migration did bear some relationship to the development of American democracy. However, in the name of rugged individualism – one of the basic tenets of the Turner thesis – many abuses were committed. The land was plundered; the "robber barons" made their appearance. At times, ruthlessness won the day; gentler qualities were not conducive to survival. This social Darwinism simply demonstrated once again – as if such proof were needed – that the strong became stronger and the weaker perished. Yet despite these negative aspects, the concept of the frontier persists in the ideology of the United States.

---

[3]   Geoffrey Gorer, *The American People; A Study in National Character*, rev. ed. (New York: Norton, 1964), p. 32.

[4]   George Wilson Pierson, "The Frontier and American Institutions", in *The Turner Thesis*, ed. George Roger Taylor (Lexington, Mass.; Heath 1972), p. 79.

[5]   "But the most important effect of the frontier has been in the promotion of democracy..."; F. J. Turner p. 51.

[6]   Benjamin F. Wright, Jr., "Political Institutions on the Frontier", in George Roger Taylor, p. 68.

APPENDIX B:
CONCERNING NATIONAL CHARACTER

Is there an American character? For some, the answer is affirmative. All they have to do is to locate and define it. It can be accounted for in the environment and in the historical experience of the United States. For others, there is more than one American character. These maintain that the environmental factor has changed, thus introducing a variable in the influence exerted. Or else the environment, at any given moment, is diverse and, consequently, affects different people in different ways, resulting in a variety of character traits.

The concept of national character in no way denies the variations of individual personality. What is claimed is that patterns of behavior ascribed to a group are exhibited by a significant number of members of that group and that these patterns have been most influential in molding the institutions of that group.[1] The inhabitants of any country may manifest a given characteristic to a greater extent than those of another country. Failure to admit this would be tantamount to denying the existence of differences between cultures.[2]

Those who have attempted to delineate so-called national traits have, in many instances, assumed that certain personality characteristics found within a given national group can be distinguished and contrasted with those of other national or ethnic groups. Such studies have been criticized because of the variations in behavior patterns that exist *within* the same group. The conclusion arrived at as a result has been that the so-called "typical" characteristic is nothing more than a stereotype which, at best, represents only a small minority of the group's members.

Yet there is another side to the coin, as stated above. It can be argued that members of a given national or ethnic group may react in a similar manner to their social environment and that, therefore, they will exhibit similar characteristics and be more like each other. This will differentiate them from other groups. One may well ask in this connection: who is performing the analysis of national characteristics and what sort of methodology is being

[1] Geoffrey Gorer, pp. 16–17.
[2] David M. Potter, p. 209.

employed? What are the intentions of the investigator and what purpose will be served by the results? Furthermore, an additional factor should be borne in mind. Even if the so-called stereotype were assumed to conform to reality, the characteristic under consideration is not etched in stone. National traits are subject to change because circumstances which mold them undergo modification.

It is reasonable to suggest that those who have dealt with the subject of the American character were undoubtedly influenced by the social and political scene which they found. These influences conditioned their commentaries. In a country as heterogeneous as the United States, marked by geographic and social diversity, it is difficult to present a reasonable picture of an authentic personality configuration. As a result, almost every conceivable trait, both positive and negative, has been attributed to the American. It is therefore not surprising to find that two categories of images, diametrically opposed to each other, have been said to typify the average North American: the individualist and idealist versus the conformist and materialist.

It is quite conceivable, for example, that the two traits, egalitarianism and individualism, ascribed to the national character, may go counter to each other. Egalitarianism can discourage individualism and vice versa. In any sort of race the runners are not expected to approach the finish line in a dead heat, just to prove that everyone is equal. Alexis de Tocqueville pointed out long ago that equality tends to regiment opinion and stifle dissent.[3] In this respect, it encourages conformity, a trait which runs counter to the spirit of individualism and which, incidentally, de Tocqueville found prevalent in the United States.

It would be interesting to compare the views of de Tocqueville with those of Thomas Jefferson within the framework of a democratic philosophy. The American President believed in the principles of liberty and equality, thus creating a model of the national character. He was an individualist who desired equality for all. Jefferson's concept of democracy was based on a vision of his countrymen as independent individualists. On the other hand, de Tocqueville's description of the American was that of an individual who was democratic but conformist, thus endangering individualism as a national characteristic.

This apparent contradiction between two versions of the American character offered by outstanding admirers of the democratic way of life would tend to cast a shadow on any attempt to generalize about national character. Yet both views seem valid. They simply prove that the North American character has undergone change; each characterization is valid for a given period in American history, each reflects a phase in the American experience. In short,

---

3   David M. Potter, p. 205.

individualism may have diminished and conformity increased as the dynamics of history unfolded.

The earlier criticism of the American character, advanced by European observers such as, for example, Mrs. Trollope and Charles Dickens, had spoken in terms of a vulgar materialism. This evolved into a negative attitude toward democratic values which were identified with American society. However, what these critics seemed to be doing was to criticize the industrialism of that society and, in the process, distort these values. The basic question that emerged as a consequence was: Could not democratic values exist in a nation that had developed from a predominantly agrarian society into one which was highly industrialized? Were industrialism and democracy basically incompatible?

The point has already been made: Turner's "Frontier Thesis" with its agrarian bias, and grounded originally in a fear of a growing industrialism, refused to go away. However, the frontier was now industrial and scientific. The notion of the frontier was deeply ingrained in the nation's thought. It represented creative responses to challenge and change, no matter where these might arise.

Conflict in values have left their imprint upon the traits ascribed to the American character. Sociological studies have described the dichotomy between individualism as expressed by the competitive drive, on the one hand, and the spirit of cooperation, on the other – both considered integral parts of the American value system.[4] The contradictory traits associated with this dichotomy, for example, kindness and generosity versus aggressive behavior in the business world, are considered by superficial observers to be typical of the American character. However, it is felt that this contradiction can be resolved by striving for material success as the only means with which to achieve all other values. What we really have here is a conflict between past ideals and present reality.[5]

Psychiatrists, too, attempted to delineate the American character. These maintained that cultural forces influenced the human personality and that, consequently, members of the same cultural group experience similar impacts and develop similar character traits. Life in the United States – so runs the argument – is frustrating and produces pressures of all kinds. The American tends to develop aggressive behavior as a means of reducing accumulated tensions. Fierce economic competition is simply an attempt to relieve one's anxiety and insecurity.[6]

4   See in this connection: Robert S. Lynd, *Knowledge for what?: The Place of Social Science in American Culture* (Princeton: Princeton University Press, 1939).

5   Thomas L. Hartshorne, p. 115.

6   The following are only two of many texts that deal with the subject: Karen Horney, *The Neurotic Personality of our Time* (New York: W. W. Norton, 1937); Erich Fromm, *Escape from Freedom* (New York: Farrar & Rinehart, 1941).

The trouble with this argument is that competition can also intensify anxiety instead of relieving it. Nevertheless the psychiatric approach has its attractive features although, once again, it is needless to point out that the practice of generalizing on the basis of individual experiences is an untenable procedure. The fact that individual patients may suffer from mental or emotional disturbances does not mean that the entire society is sick.

APPENDIX C:
CONCERNING THE PURITANS AND PURITANISM

The evolving conception of American characteristics is further illustrated by an examination of a significant strand in the fabric of the national personality. Many are critical commentaries concerning the influence of the Puritan strain on the formation of the American character, commentaries which have themselves shown considerable variation, especially in the twentieth century. Perhaps this is due to the fact that the essence of Puritanism has undergone modification; moreover, the American social panorama itself has experienced change.

In the matter of definitions, Perry Miller, a foremost authority on the subject of Puritanism, has stated: "Puritanism may be defined empirically as that point of view or code of values, carried to New England by the first settlers...The New Englanders established Puritanism...as one of the continuous factors in American life and thought."[1]

Puritanism was subject to the dynamics of social change. As the centuries wore on, it bore little resemblance to what it had been in the seventeenth century. In fact, one outstanding philosopher maintained that even though it had been an intellectual tradition originally, it gradually became a mental and emotional attitude distinguished by its overwhelming practicality.[2] The former emphasis on education, religion and literature was replaced by moral compulsiveness and conformity. Twentieth-century critics maintained that Puritanism was inimical to cultural activity. For example, H. L. Mencken identified Puritanism with hypocrisy and witch-hunting. James Truslow Adams was repelled by the bigotry and intolerance of the Puritans. V. L. Parrington saw Puritanism as contrary to the American progressive tradition.[3] However, since the 1920s historians have taken a second look and have revised earlier prejudicial conceptions. They now realize that the respect for learning manifested by the Puritans was an admirable quality and that the latter were not ignorant bigots.

If there is one character trait that has been preserved throughout the

---

[1]   Quoted by Richard Schlatter, "The Puritan Strain", in *The Reconstruction of American History*, ed. John Higham (London: Hutchinson, 1962), pp. 28–29.
[2]   George Santayana, quoted in Hartshorne, p. 87.
[3]   Richard Schlatter, pp. 30–31.

139

centuries, it is individualism. Although the early Puritan conception of God was authoritarian, the Puritan nevertheless held that the believer should interpret the Bible for himself. He thus stressed the responsibility of the individual to exercise his own intelligence. In this respect the individualism of the Puritan can be said to coincide with the self-reliance of another traditional figure in American society, namely, the Pioneer. The latter's concern with material problems coincided harmoniously with the Puritan's attitude.

The centrality of self-reliance common to both Puritanism and the Pioneer spirit was conductive to the fostering of a democratic ethos. In short, Puritanism and Democracy both respected the individual.[4] Then, too, the emphasis on material values as a character trait cannot be brushed aside. This aspect of the national character as exemplified by the American business man also finds its place in Puritan doctrine. Thrift and industry were the characteristics of a good Puritan. The self-made man who engaged in activities which proved profitable was merely serving God's will.[5]

---

[4] Ralph Barton Perry, *Puritanism and Democracy* (New York: The Vanguard Press, 1944), p. 192.
[5] Ralph Barton Perry, p. 213.

APPENDIX D:
CONCERNING U.S. INTERVENTION

The basic question that should be asked in connection with U.S. intervention is: does Washington intervene in order to promote and strengthen democracy as it claims, or rather to maintain what it considers to be "stability" in the hemisphere? An anti-democratic, authoritarian regime, one which does not threaten U.S. interests, is not likely to incur the antagonism of the United States. If such a regime should turn out to be a threat, then it becomes easier to intervene in the name of democracy. Conversely, if a more liberal democratic government were to replace a right-wing regime, and be perceived as potentially inimical to U.S. strategic interests, would the United States attempt to destabilize such government and intervene under the cloak of advancing the cause of democracy?

U.S. intervention in the past has always left a bad taste. Latin Americans are suspicious every time Washington moves to "control" a situation. Their perception, unfortunately, takes it for granted that the more interventionist the U.S. has been, the less able it has been to encourage democratic policies.[1]

The policy of intervention must be reexamined. Supporting military dictators in the name of maintaining stability must be replaced by concern for human rights. Obsolete regimes that violate these rights should not receive any support. The image of the United States is lamentably a negative one. It is an image associated with opposition to progressive change.

The last decade of the twentieth century is replete with challenges. The United States may have to take risks which it has hitherto been reluctant to assume. It may be necessary to support liberal and leftist parties as a lever against authoritarian right-wing elements, yet guarding against the establishment of a new authoritarianism.[2] This will prove to be an exercise requiring extreme diplomatic skills. Can the United States manage this basic change in approach and attitude? The United States must present a more human face to counteract the impression that it is insensitive to the needs of

---

[1] Abraham F. Lowenthal, "The United States and Latin American Democracy: Learning from History", in A. F. Lowenthal, *Exporting Democracy: The United States and Latin America* (Baltimore: The Johns Hopkins University Press, 1991), p. 260.

[2] Tom J. Farer, *The Grand Strategy of the United States in Latin America* (New Brunswick, N.J.: Transition Books, 1988), p. 231.

the people of Latin America. Perhaps it would be more effective to work with non-governmental organizations to support the democratic process and help effect positive changes in land reform, housing, education and social welfare.[3]

A more effective program, designed to handle problems such as illegal drugs, bank debts and immigration can be much more salutary than talk of subversive movements. In fact, a greater measure of tolerance of more liberal or even radical governments might conceivably build up more sympathy and good will among Spanish Americans, and reduce the appeal and effectiveness of guerilla movements. The people of Latin America, not just the government bureaucrats, must be made aware – and the media have a responsible task in this respect – that the United States is a liberal democracy and that it will act in accordance with its libertarian ethos.[4]

---

[3] Michael J. Kryzanek, 2nd ed. *U.S.-Latin American Relations* (New York: Praeger, 1990), p. 236.
[4] Tom J. Farer, p. 245.

APPENDIX E:
CONCERNING DEPENDENCY AND UNDERDEVELOPMENT

Innumerable volumes have dealt with the subject of underdevelopment and dependency in Latin America. Many writers see a link between the domestic factors to be found in a given state and the external factors, e.g., the presence of a foreign capitalist nation seeking possibilities for investments. Some writers are more interested in explaining international relations, while others concentrate on problems of underdevelopment. Those who view dependency as a problem involving a power relationship between two nation-states, consider the possibility of negotiations between them. On the other hand, the more radical view holds that dependency on a foreign country is a function of capitalism, and that in order to put an end to dependency and underdevelopment, it is necessary to eliminate the capitalist system.

Of course, the relationship between external and internal forces is not uniform for the Latin American continent as a whole. Many variations exist, depending on the differences in capitalist expansion in various countries, the diversity of resources and the degree of cooperation or opposition vis-à-vis foreign interests, manifested by local, national groups and social classes. Against this background the development of the Latin American states depends upon "how successful local social classes have been in participating in the production process and in setting up institutional controls to insure that participation".[1]

Rodolfo Stavenhagen spells this out in greater detail, outlining three alternatives for solving the present conditions of the continent. The first envisages the continuation of the existing state of dependency. Various Latin American countries, at different stages of underdevelopment, will experience periodic crises. This viewpoint is supported by the multinational corporations and by political and military strategy. In addition, one must not forget certain elements of the native socio-economic groups whose class interests dictate opposition to basic change in the economic structure.

A second possibility which has not been too successful involves the political activization of popular social classes, inspired by a nationalist ideology.

---

[1] Fernando Henrique Cardoso and Enzo Faletto, *Dependency and Development in Latin America* (Berkeley, California: University of California Press, 1979), p. 29.

A broad alliance of this sort within the context of State capitalism, involving political parties, military groups and government technocrats, would carry out tasks in an attempt to reduce dependency, but without destroying the present class structure. This broad alliance would have to negotiate with foreign interests and limit the power of the dominant social classes. To this end it would be necessary to enlist the support of the masses, and simultaneously oppose any attempt by the political left to seize power.

The third alternative, which is what the second option strives to prevent, is the socialist model which has had and continues to experience more failures than successes. The most difficult step under this program is putting an end to the control by multinational corporations. This, it is hoped, will break external dependency, eliminate marginality and internal colonialism, redistribute income, and raise the standard of living of the population.[2]

Several basic questions might be asked at this point: What type of development will prevail if the socio-economic structure is changed? What kind of system will result? Will socialism be a satisfactory substitute? What sort of socialism? Totalitarian? Democratic?[3]

[2] Rodolfo Stavenhagen, "The Future of Latin America: Between Underdevelopment and Revolution", in *From Dependency to Development*, ed. Heraldo Muñoz (Boulder, Colorado: Westview Press, 1981), pp. 220–21.

[3] Heraldo Muñoz, "The Various Roads to Development", in Heraldo Muñoz, ed. pp. 1–10.

LIST OF WORKS CONSULTED

Abellán, José Luis. *La idea de América*: *idea y evolución*. Madrid: Istmo, 1972.

Adamic, Louis. *From Many Lands*. New York: Harper, 1940.

Alba, Victor. "Nationalism and Political Reality", *Americas*, 18, No. 17 (1968), pp. 571–74.

———. *Nationalists Without Nations*. New York: Frederick A. Praeger Publishers, 1968.

Alberdi, Juan Bautista. "Bases...", in *Antología del Pensamiento Social y Politico de América Latina*, ed. Leopoldo Zea, Washington, D.C. Unión Panamericana, 1964.

———. *Proceso a Sarmiento*. Buenos Aires: Ediciones Caldea, 1967.

Allen, David H. Jr., "Rubén Darío frente a la creciente influencia de los Estados Unidos", *Revista Iberoamericana*. 33, No. 64 (1967), pp. 387–93.

Arango Cano, Jesús. *Estados Unidos, mito y realidad*. Bogotá: Librería Voluntad, 1959.

Arciniegas, Germán. *Este pueblo de América*. México: Fondo de Cultura Económica, 1945.

Arévalo Juan José. *The Shark and the Sardines*. New York: L. Stuart, 1961.

Arguedas, Alcides. *Pueblo enfermo*. 3rd ed. La Paz: Ediciones "Puerta del Sol", 1936.

Asturias, Miguel Angel. *Viento fuerte*. Buenos Aires: Editorial Losada, 1950.

Balseiro, José Agustín, "Estudios Rubendarianos: Arieles y Calibanes", *Revista Hispánica Moderna*, 31, Nos. 1–4, Jan.–Oct. (1965), pp. 46–53.

———. *Expresión de Hispanoamérica*. 2nd rev. ed. Madrid: Editorial Gredos, 1970.

Barahona Jiménez, Luis, "Hispanoamérica en el pensamiento de José Ortega y Gasset", *Revista de Filosofía de la Universidad de Costa Rica*, 7, No. 25 (1969), pp. 153–62.

Bar-Lewaw Mulstock, I. *José Vasconcelos, Vida y obra*. México: Clásica Selecta Editora Librería, 1965.

Basarde, Jorge. *Excelsior*, Lima, June–July 1942.

Bello, Andrés, "La Confederacion de Hispanoamérica", in *Bello*. Ed. Gabriel Méndez Plancarte, México: Ediciones de la Secretaría de Educación Pública, 1943, pp. 84–88.

Bilbao, Francisco. *El evangelio americano*. Santiago: Ediciones Ercilla, 1941.

Bolívar, Simón. *His Basic Thoughts*, Ed. Manuel Pérez Vila. Caracas: Academia Nacional de la Historia, 1980.

———. Speech at the Congress of Venezuela, Feb. 13, 1819. Trans. by J. Hamilton. Caracas: Cromotip C.A., 1974.

Boorstin, Daniel J. *America and the Image of Europe*. New York: The World Publication Co. 1960.

Briceño Guerrero, J. M. "Unidad y diversidad de Latinoamérica", in *Anuario, Latino América*. México: UNAM 2, 1969, pp. 161–68.

Brogan, D. W. *The American Character*. New York: Alfred A. Knopf, 1950.

Bruckberger, R. L. *Image of America*. New York: The Viking Press, 1959.

Bryce, James. "The True Faults of American Democracy", in Henry Steele Commager, *America in Perspective*. New York: Random House, 1947, pp. 188–214.

Caballero Calderón, Eduardo. *Obras*. Medellín, Colombia: Editorial Bedout, 1963.

Castro, Américo, *Iberoamérica*. 3rd ed. New York: Holt, Rinehart and Winston, 1954.

Commager, Henry Steele, ed. *America in Perspective*. New York: Random House, 1947.

Commager, Henry Steele and Elmo Giordanetti, *Was America a Mistake?* Columbia, South Carolina: University of South Carolina Press, 1967.

Cosío Villegas, Daniel. "Los problemas de América", in José Luis Martínez, *El ensayo mexicano moderno*. México: Fondo de Cultura Económica 1958, 1, pp. 471–92.

Craig, G. Dundas, *The Modernist Trend in Spanish-American Poetry*. Berkeley: University of California Press, 1934.

Crawford, William R. *A Century of Latin American Thought*. Cambridge, Mass. Harvard University Press, 1945.

Crevecoeur, Michel Guillaume Jean de. "What is an American?", in Henry Steele Commager, *America in Perspective*. New York: Random House, 1947, pp. 26–38.

Current History, vol. 87, March 1988.

Darío, Rubén. "To Roosevelt", in G. Dundas Craig, *The Modernist Trend in Spanish-American Poetry*. Berkeley: University of California Press, 1934, pp. 69–71.

Delano, Luis Enrique. ed. *Lastarria*. México: Ediciones de la Secretaría de Educación Pública. 1944.

De Soto, Hernando. *The Other Path*. New York: Harper & Row, 1989.

Díaz-Plaja, Guillermo. *Hispanoamérica en su literatura*. Navarra: Salvat Editores, S.A. 1972.

Dickey, J. S. and W. H. Shepardson. *Canada and the American Presence*. New York: New York University Press. 1975.

Díez de Medina, Fernando. "Europa y América, dos polos culturales", in Ernesto Mejía Sánchez, *El ensayo actual latinoamericano*. México: Ediciones de Andrea, 1971, pp. 39–43.

Echeverría, Esteban. *Dogma Socialista*. La Plata: 1940.

English, H. Edward, ed. *Canada-U.S. Relations*. New York: Praeger Publishers, 1976.

Fals Borda, Orlando, "Sentido actual de la identidad cultural", in *Cuadernos americanos*, México, 239, No. 6 (1981), pp. 18–22.

Farer, Tom J. *The Grand Strategy of the United States in Latin America*, New Brunswick, N.J.: Transition Books, 1988.

Feijoo y Montenegro, Benito Jerónimo, *Dos discursos de Feijoo*. Ed. Agustín Millares Carlo, México: Secretaría de Educación, Publica, 1945.

Fernández Retamar, Roberto. *Calibán cannibale*. Paris: François Maspero, 1973.

Francovich, Guillermo. "Pachamama", in *Antología de Filosofía Americana Contemporánea*, Ed. Leopoldo Zea. México: Costa-Amic, 1968, pp. 79–87.

Frank, Waldo. *Primer mensaje a la América hispana*. Madrid: Revista de Occidente, 1929.

———. *El redescubrimiento de América*. 2nd ed. Madrid: Revista de Occidente, 1930.

Gaos, José. *Filosofía mexicana de nuestros días*. México: Imprenta Universitaria, 1954.

———. *En torno a la filosofía mexicana*. México. Alianza Editorial Mexicana, 1980.

García Morente, Manuel. *Idea de la hispanidad*. Madrid: Espasa-Calpe, S.A. 1961.

Gerbi, Antonello. *The Dispute of the New World: the History of a Polemic*. Pittsburgh: The University of Pittsburgh Press, 1973.

Glazer, Nathan. *Ethnic Dilemmas*. Cambridge, Mass.: Harvard University Press, 1983.

Gómez Martínez, J. L. and F. J. Pinedo, eds. *Los Ensayistas*. Athens, Georgia: University of Georgia, 1987–88.

Gómez Robledo, Antonio. *Idea y experiencia de América*. México: Fondo de Cultura Económica, 1958.

González Prada, Manuel. "Españoles y Yankees", in *Conciencia intelectual de América*, ed. Carlos Ripoll. New York: Las Américas Publishing Co. 1966, pp. 205–08.

Gorer, Geoffrey. *The American People: A Study in National Character*, rev. ed. New York: W. W. Norton and Co., 1964.

Gumucio, Mario Baptista. *Latinoamericanos y Norteamericanos*. La Paz: Editorial "Artística", 1986.

Gutiérrez Girodet, Rafael. *La imagen de América en Alfonso Reyes*. Madrid: Insula, 1955.

Haley, Alex. *Roots*. Garden City, N.Y.: Doubleday, 1976.

Hanke, Lewis. *Do the Americans Have a Common History?* New York: Alfred A. Knopf, 1964.

Hartshorne, Thomas L. *The Distorted Image*. Cleveland: The Press of Case Western Reserve University, 1968.

Hegel, Georg W. F. *Lectures on the Philosophy of History*. Trans. by H. B. Nesbit. Cambridge: Cambridge University Press, 1975.

Henríquez Ureña, Pedro. *La Utopía de América*. Caracas: Biblioteca Ayacucho, 1978.

Henry, William A. III. "Beyond the Melting Pot", *Time*, April 9, 1990.

Herring, Hubert. *A History of Latin America – From the Beginning to the Present*. New York: Alfred A. Knopf, 1961.

Higham, John. *The Reconstruction of American History*. London: Hutchinson University Library, 1963.

———. *Historia de la literatura argentina: Los contemporáneos*. Buenos Aires: Centro Editor de América Latina, 3, 1968.

Hostos, Eugenio Maria de. "El día de América", in *Conciencia intelectual de América*. Ed. Carlos Ripoll. New York: Las Américas Publishing Co. 1966, pp. 150–56.

———. *Obras Completas. La cuna de América*, Havana: Cultural, S.A. 1939.

————. *Obras Completas. España y América*, Paris: Ediciones Literarias y Artísticas, 1954.

————. *Obras Completas. Temas Sudamericanos*. Havana: Cultura, S.A. 1939.

Kallen, Horace. *Culture and Democracy in the United States: Studies in the Group Psychology of the American People*. New York: 1924.

Keyserling, Count Hermann. *South American Meditations*. New York: Harper and Bros., 1932.

Kohn, Hans. *Nationalism: Its Meaning and History*. New York: D. Van Nostrand Co. Inc., 1965.

Kryzanek, Michael J. *U.S.-Latin American Relations*, 2nd ed. New York: Praeger Publishers, 1990.

Lafaye, Jacques, "Los abismos de la identidad cultural", in *Past and Present in the Americas*. Ed. John Lynch. Manchester: Manchester University Press, 1982.

Laín Entralgo, Pedro. *España como problema*. Madrid: Aguilar, 1957.

Lama, George de. "Latin World on the Edge of an Abyss", *Chicago Tribune*, June 4, 1989.

Lastarria, José Victorino. "Europa Autoritaria y Europa Democrática", in *Lastarria*, ed. Luis Enrique Délano. México: Ediciones de la Secretaría de Educación Pública, 1944.

Leal, Luis. "A Spanish American Perspective of Anglo-American Literature", *Revista Canadiense de Estudios Hispánicos*. Toronto: 5, No. 1 (1980), pp. 61–73.

Lipp, Solomon. *Leopoldo Zea: From "Mexicanidad" to a Philosophy of History*. Waterloo, Ontario: Wilfrid Laurier University Press, 1980.

————. "Racial and Ethnic Problems: Perú", in *International Journal of Group Tensions*, 19, No. 4 (1989), pp. 339–48.

Lowenthal, Abraham F. *Exporting Democracy: The United States and Latin America*. Baltimore: The Johns Hopkins University Press, 1991.

Lumsden, Jan, ed. *The Americanization of Canada*. Toronto: University of Toronto Press, 1991.

Lynch, John, ed. *Past and Present in the Americas*. Manchester: Manchester University Press, 1982.

Lynd, Robert S. *Knowledge for What? The Place of Social Science in American Culture*. Princeton: Princeton University Press, 1939.

Mackay, Alexander, "Every American is an Apostle of the Democratic Creed", in Henry Steele Commager. *America in Perspective*. New York: Random House, 1947, pp. 108–19.

MacLean's July 3, 1989.

MacLean's October 16, 1989.

Maclean's January 1, 1990.

MacLean's June 25, 1990.

Madariaga, Salvador de. *Essays with a Purpose*. London: Hollis and Carter, 1954.

————. *Obras escogidas: ensayos*. Buenos Aires: Editorial Sudamericana, 1972.

Mallea, Eduardo. *Historia de una pasión argentina*. 6th ed. Madrid: Espasa-Calpe, 1969.

————. *La vida blanca*. Buenos Aires: Sur, 1960.

Mañach, Jorge. "El Quijotismo y América", in *El ensayo actual latinoamericano*. Ed. E. Mejía Sánchez and F. Guillén, México: Ediciones de Andrea, 1971, pp. 93–100.

Martí, José. "Nuestra América", in *Conciencia intelectual de América*. Ed. Carlos Ripoll. New York: Las Américas Publishing Co. 1966.

———. "La verdad sobre los Estados Unidos", in *Páginas escogidas*. Havana: Instituto Cubano del Libro, 1971, pp. 387–92.

Martínez, José Luis. *El ensayo mexicano moderno*. México: Fondo de Cultura Económica, 1958.

Martínez Estrada, Ezequiel. *Radiografía de la Pampa*, 5th ed. Buenos Aires: Editorial Losada, S.A. 1953.

Mays Vallenilla, Ernesto, "El problema de América", in *Antología de la Filosofía Americana Contemporánea*. México: B. Costa Amic, 1968, pp. 205–37.

Mejía Sánchez, E. and F. Guillén, ed. *El ensayo actual latinoamericano*. México: Ediciones de Andrea, 1971.

Méndez Plancarte, Gabriel, ed. *Bello*, México: Ediciones de la Secretaría Pública, 1943.

Mitre y Vedia, Bartolomé. In a letter, concerning Sarmiento, dated Sept. 10, 1886, and published in *La Nación* of Buenos Aires.

Molina, Enrique. *Confesión filosófica y llamado de superación a la América Hispana*. Santiago: Editorial Nascimento, 1942.

Montalvo, Juan. "La hermosura invisible", in *Conciencia intelectual de América*. Ed. Carlos Ripoll. New York: Las Américas Publishing Co., 1966.

Müller-Freienfels, Richard. "The Mechanization and Standardization of American Life", in Henry Steele Commager, *America in Perspective*. New York: Random House, 1947, pp. 272–79.

Muñoz, Heraldo, ed. *From Dependency to Development*. Boulder, Colorado: Westview Press, 1981.

Neustadt, Bernardo. *La Argentina y los Argentinos*. Buenos Aires: Emccé Editores, 1976.

O'Gorman, Edmundo. *La idea del descubrimiento de América*. México: Centro de Estudios Filosóficos, 1951.

Onís, José de. *The United States as seen by Spanish American Writers*. New York: Gordian Press, 1975.

Ortega y Gasset, José. *En torno a Galileo*. Madrid: Espasa-Calpe, 1965.

———. *Obras Completas*, 2nd ed. Madrid: Revista de Occidente, Vol. II, 1950.

Paz, Octavio. "El espejo indiscreto", in *El ogro filantrópico*. México: Editorial Joaquín Mortiz, 1979.

———. *El laberinto de la soledad*, 3rd ed. México: Fondo de Cultura Económica, 1963.

———. *The Labyrinth of Solitude*. Trans. by Lysandro Kemp. New York: Grove Press, 1961.

———. *El ogro filantrópico*. México: Editorial Joaquín Mortiz, 1979.

———. *Tiempo nublado*. Barcelona: Editorial Seix Barral, 1983.

Pérez Vila, Manuel, ed. *Simón Bolívar: His Basic Thoughts*. Caracas: Academia Nacional de la Historia, 1980.

Perry, Ralph Barton, *Puritanism and Democracy*. New York: The Vanguard Press, 1944.

Peterson, William et al. *Concepts of Ethnicity*. Cambridge, Mass.: Harvard University Press, 1982.

Pinedo, Javier, "La Ensayística y el problema de la identidad", in *Los Ensayistas*.

Ed. J. L. Gómez Martínez and F. J. Pinedo. Athens, Ga.: University of Georgia, 1987–88, pp. 22–25.

Piper, Anson C. "El Yankee en las obras de Gallegos", *Hispania*, 33, No. 4 (1950) pp. 328–41.

Quintanilla, Luis. *A Latin American Speaks*. New York: The MacMillan Co., 1943.

Rama, Carlos M. *La imagen de los Estados Unidos en la América Latina*. México: Sep Diana, 1975.

Ramos, Samuel. *El perfil del hombre y la cultura en México*, 5th ed. México: Espasa-Calpe Mexicana. 1972.

Rangel, Carlos. *Del buen salvaje al buen revolucionario*. Caracas: Monte Avila, Editores, 1976.

Redekop, John, ed. *The Star-Spangled Banner*, Toronto: Peter Martin Associates, Ltd., 1971.

Reid, John T. "The Rise and Decline of the Ariel-Calibán Antithesis in Spanish America", *The Americas*, 34, No. 3 (1978), pp. 345–55.

Reyes, Alfonso. "Ultima Tule", in *Conciencia Intelectual de América*. Ed. Carlos Ripoll. New York: Las Américas Publishing Company, 1966.

Ribero, Darcy. *The Americans and Civilization*. New York: E. P. Dutton and Co., Inc., 1971.

Ripoll, Carlos. *Conciencia intelectual de América*. New York: Las Américas Publishing Company, 1966.

Rodó, José Enrique. *Ariel*, 1st ed. Buenos Aires: Espasa-Calpe, 1948.

Rodríguez Monegal, Emir. "Las metamorfosis de Calibán", *Vuelta*, México, 3, no. 25 (1978), p. 25.

Rodríguez Vega, Eugenio. *Apuntes para una sociología costarricense*. San José: Edición Universitaria, 1953.

———. "Debe y Haber del Hombre Costarricense", *Revista de la Universidad de Costa Rica*, San José, No. 10 (1954), pp. 9–32.

Rojas, Ricardo. *Blasón de plata*. Buenos Aires: Editorial Losada, 1941.

Sábato, Ernesto. *La cultura en la encrucijada nacional*. Buenos Aires: Editorial Sudamericana, 1976.

Sacks, Norman P. "José Victorino Lastarria y Henry Thomas Buckle: El Positivismo, La Historia de España", in *Estudios sobre José Victorino Lastarria*. Santiago: Ediciones de la Universidad de Chile, 1988, pp. 124–51.

Sacuto, Antonio. "El indio en la obra literaria de Sarmiento y Martí", *Cuadernos Americanos*, México: 156 (Jan.–Feb. 1968), pp. 137–63.

Sánchez, Luis Alberto. *Examen espectral de América Latina*, 2nd ed. Buenos Aires: Editorial Losada, 1962.

———. "A New Interpretation of the History of America", *The Hispanic American Historical Review*, No. 23 (1943), pp. 441–56.

Sarmiento, Domingo, F. "Conflicto y armonías de las razas en América", in *Obras*, 5th ed. Buenos Aires: Espasa-Calpe, 1939.

———. *Facundo*. Buenos Aires: Editorial Losada, 1938.

Sierra, Justo, "Epistolario y papeles privados", in *Obras Completas*. México; UNAM. 1977, 14.

———. "Viajes en tierra", in *Obras Completas*. México; UNAM. 1977, 6.

Slavin, Arthur J., "The American Principle from More to Locke", in *Image of America*. Ed. R. L. Bruckberger, New York: Viking Press, 1959.

Stabb, Martin S. *In Quest of Identity*. Chapel Hill: University of North Carolina Press, 1967.

Starobin, Joseph. *Paris to Peking*. New York: Cameron Associates, 1955.

Stavehagen, Rodolfo. "The Future of Latin America: Between Underdevelopment and Revolution", in *From Dependency to Development*. Ed. Heraldo Muñoz. Boulder, Colorado: Westview Press, 1981, pp. 207–23.

Steele, J. and R. Mathews. "The Universities and the Mind", in *The Americanization of Canada*. Ed. Jan Lumsden, Toronto: University of Toronto Press, 1960.

Subercasseaux, Benjamín, "Visión de Estados Unidos y América en la Elite Liberal (1860–70)", in *Cuadernos Americanos* (México) 130, No. 3 (May–June, 1980), pp. 119–33.

Taylor, George Roger, ed. *The Turner Thesis*. Lexington, Mass.: D. C. Heath and Co., 1972.

Tocqueville, Alexis de. *Democracy in America*. New York: Alfred A. Knopf, Vintage Books, 1945, vol. I.

Trollope, Frances. "Domestic Manners of the Americans", in Antonello Gerbi, *The Dispute of the New World: The History of a Polemic (1759–1900)*. Pittsburgh: The University of Pittsburgh Press, 1973, pp. 473–79.

Trottier, R. G. et al., ed. *Conference on Canadian-American Affairs*. Boston: Ginn and Co., 1937.

Turner, Frederick Jackson. *The Significance of the Frontier in American History*. New York: Frederick Ungar Publishing Co., 1963.

Unamuno, Miguel de. "La envidia hispánica", in *Mi religión y otros ensayos*, 4th ed. Madrid: Espasa-Calpe, 1964, pp. 42–49.

Urbanski, Edmund Stephen. *Hispanoamérica, sus razas y civilizaciones*. New York: Eliseo Torres & Sons. 1972.

Valenzuela, Victor M. *Anti-United States Sentiment in Latin American Literature and Other Essays*. Bethlehem, Pa., 1982.

Vargas Llosa, Mario. "La amistad difícil", *Ideas*, University of Miami, 2, No. 1 (1988), pp. 1–8.

Vasconcelos, José. *Indología, una interpretación de la cultura iberoamericana*. Paris: Agencia Mundial de Librería, p. 197.

Villegas, Abelardo. *Autognosis: el pensamiento mexicano en el siglo XX*. México: Instituto Panamericano de Geografía e Historia, 1985.

———. *Cultura y politica en América Latina*. México: Editorial Extemporáneos, 1978.

———. *La filosofía de lo mexicano*. México: Fondo de Cultura Económica, 1960.

Weinstein, Michael A. "Lamento y Utopía: Respuestas al Imperio Norteamericano en George Grant y Leopoldo Zea", in *Nuestra América*, México: UNAM, 3, No. 8 (1983), pp. 145–59.

Woodward, W. E. *A New American History*. New York: The Literary Guild, 1937.

Zavala, Silvio. "la 'Utopía' de Tomás Moro en la Nueva España", in *El ensayo mexicano moderno*. Vol. II. Ed. José Luis Martínez. México: Fondo de Cultura Económica, 1958.

Zea, Leopoldo. *América como conciencia*. México: Ediciones Cuadernos Americanos, 1953.

———. *Antología de Filosofía Americana Contemporánea*. México: B. Costa-Amic, 1968.

————. *Dependencia y liberación en la cultura latinoamericana*. México: Cuadernos de Joaquín Mortiz, 1974.

————. *Latin America and the World*. Norman, Oklahoma: University of Oklahoma Press, 1969.

————. *Precursores del pensamiento latinoamericano contemporáneo*. México: Sep Diana, 1970.

Zea, Leopoldo and Abelardo Villegas, ed. *Antología del pensamiento social y político de América Latina*. Washington, D.C.: Unión Panamericana, 1964.

Zum Felde, Alberto, *El problema de la cultura en América*. Buenos Aires: Losada, 1943.

INDEX